SURVIVING A MASSA

"Having read *Surviving a Massacre, Rampage, or Spree Killing* by Professor Arthur Cohen, I find it brings some sense to a very complex issue facing America. I feel strongly that this book should be on the desk of any administrator who is responsible for the safety of our citizens and children. At a minimum, this should be the textbook for a mandated course involving law enforcement, our educators, government officials, and elected officials."

Deputy Chief Charles Mader (retired)
is a nationally recognized trainer
and use-of-force expert. He has experience
as a detective commander, operations commander,
and deputy chief.

"This book is one of the most comprehensive texts ever written on the subject of rampage killing. The chapters explore the how, why, where, and what you can do to survive these kinds of attacks."

Joseph J. Truncale is an advisory board member of the
International Law Enforcement Educators
and Trainers Association, law enforcement trainer,
author of more than 50 books/manuals in the martial arts,
police defensive tactics, and survival fields.

"Professor Cohen provides a shocking and provocative look into these extremely rare yet catastrophic events. *Surviving a Massacre, Rampage, or Spree Killing* provides a global view of these horrific events, which his work shows can occur in any community in the world."

Michael Dorn is a school safety specialist,
the executive director of Safe Havens, and the former
chief of police for Bibb County, Georgia, public schools.
He is also the author of Innocent Targets: When Terrorism Comes to School.

i

PRAISE FOR
SURVIVING A MASSACRE, RAMPAGE, OR SPREE KILLING

"Professor Arthur Cohen, a highly regarded and internationally respected martial artist, teacher, lecturer, and author, has produced another outstanding contribution to the field of personal survival. In this volume, *Surviving a Massacre, Rampage, or Spree Killing,* Professor Cohen has painstakingly researched, analyzed, and offered suggestions to avoid, plan for, and live through these kinds of attacks. He addresses such issues as individual actions that can help you and your family, friends, and others deal with overt and covert violence. He also provides concrete suggestions for educators, law enforcement officers, and policymakers to help prevent and successfully respond to attacks of this nature. This is a book that should be in the library of anyone who is concerned with his/her personal safety and of those who are most important to him/her."

Ron Kazoroski, police chief (retired),
is a former police chief/public safety director,
police academy director, defensive tactics instructor,
and University of Central Florida self-defense instructor.

"*Surviving a Massacre, Rampage, or Spree Killing* should be required reading for every teacher and administrator in education. Professor Cohen's insight into the problems of young people and the gang culture is on target. The chapters on education give detailed information on the mind-set of disturbed youth, the red flags to look for, and possible causes for the youngster's behavior, including why and how gangs have the influence they have over our youth. Anyone who works in education, especially in the inner cities, can gain valuable information from reading Professor Cohen's book."

Alex Emerling, the former assistant principal
at the New York City Department of Education,
is an adjunct lecturer at NYC College of Technology.

ii

SURVIVING A MASSACRE, RAMPAGE, OR SPREE KILLING

SURVIVING A MASSACRE, RAMPAGE, OR SPREE KILLING

Arthur Cohen

PALADIN PRESS • BOULDER, COLORADO

Surviving a Massacre, Rampage, or Spree Killing
by Arthur Cohen

Copyright © 2010 by Arthur Cohen

ISBN 13: 978-1-58160-725-3
Printed in the United States of America

Published by Paladin Press, a division of
Paladin Enterprises, Inc.
Gunbarrel Tech Center
7077 Winchester Circle
Boulder, Colorado 80301 USA, +1.303.443.7250

Direct inquiries and/or orders to the above address.

PALADIN, PALADIN PRESS, and the "horse head" design
are trademarks belonging to Paladin Enterprises and
registered in United States Patent and Trademark Office.

Visit our website at www.paladin-press.com

TABLE OF
CONTENTS

WARNING

Some of the techniques covered in this book are extremely dangerous, but given the circumstances under which they might be employed, their inclusion is justified. However, you should be trained in the techniques before trying to employ them. This book is no substitute for professional instruction in firearms handling and disarms, and in various elements of self-defense. Many of the recommendations require that you be physically fit and in good health. It is your responsibility to make sure that you are. Additionally, none of the information in this book should be considered as legal advice. If you have any questions about what constitutes legal actions, please consult an attorney.

Neither the author nor the publisher assumes any responsibility for the use or misuse of information contained herein. It is presented *for academic study only*.

ACKNOWLEDGMENTS

Any time a product is produced or something is invented, a name goes with it. Often there are many others behind the scene who have either made a contribution or had an impact on that work. It could be in the form of encouragement, inspiration, or knowledge. This is definitely the case with this book, and many of the people who provided this help or support aren't even aware of their contribution.

First, I would like to thank my mother and father, Rachel and Aaron Cohen, for their love, my work ethic, and their encouragement for me to be the best that I could be at whatever I do. This did not mean I was destined to be a world champion at anything. It just meant I should put 100 percent into what I do and work to my potential. Thanks.

My first martial arts instructor, Grand Master Dr. Rhin Moon Chun, impacted my life greatly. He introduced me to tae kwon do and started me on my martial arts odyssey. This journey connected me with some extraordinary martial artists along the way, some well known and some not. There are many great martial artists who do their thing quietly behind the scenes. I greatly appreciate the information they all shared.

I must also acknowledge Hunter College and Stony Brook University, where I went to school. The information I gathered in my study of biology, animal behavior, psychology, and engineering was extremely useful in understanding many of the topics I researched for this book, including combat, stress, pressure points, the workings of the human mind, and personal safety. At the time, I had no inkling how important this information would be to me.

In the early 1980s, I became involved with the law enforcement community, locally with the Nassau County Sheriff's Department and then nationally with the Justice System Training Association (JSTA). I made many friends within the JSTA and later established friendships with members of the American Society of Law Enforcement Trainers (ASLET), the International Law Enforcement Educators and Trainers Association (ILEETA), and the *Defensive Tactics Newsletter*. Over an almost 30-year period, I attended seminars with several hundred very talented law enforcement instructors and got a "real" education. I was inspired to read everything I could get my hands on by many great professionals. From these instructors and friends, I was able to acquire a vast amount of knowledge concerning the subject of violence and personal safety.

As a former member of the National Speakers Association, I was inspired by some greats to improve my speaking. Now my wife says I can't shut up.

One might wonder why not many names are given. There are so many, it would take pages. Plus, I might inadvertently leave someone out, and I wouldn't want to do that. Thanks to all, and I greatly value your friendship.

I would also like to thank Adam Gordon, Richard Rosenzweig, and Ron Kazoroski for volunteering to help me dot the i's and cross the t's in this book.

Lastly, I appreciate the opportunity Paladin Press has provided me to reach out to so many.

AUTHOR'S NOTES

Before telling you what this book is, I thought it best to tell you what it isn't. After careful thought, terrorism, gang murders, family annihilations, and serial murders were excluded from this study. All these topics are forms of mass murder, and there are certainly areas of overlap with spree killings. Where relevant, I have discussed these common characteristics. But terrorism, gang murder, family annihilation, and serial murder each has a distinct dynamic, with its own sets of causes and solutions, that makes it very different than a spree killing or rampage. In the end, the differences seemed more significant than the similarities. Including these topics would have made this book much longer and less focused. Each is worthy of its own study, as they are major issues facing our society.

I gave a lot of thought to whether the information contained in this book would be helpful to a potential shooter. It is my opinion there is very little information contained here that could benefit the shooter, and a lot that might be of benefit to the rest of us.

One of my pet peeves is all the self-described "experts" who profess to know all there is to know about a subject and offer their advice to any and every one, regardless of its validity. So I use the term "expert" carefully throughout this book. It is up to you to determine whether an "expert" is really expert at his topic before following his advice. This takes research on your part, sometimes a lot of it.

Spree killers, though predominantly male, come in both genders, as do their victims, teachers, cops, and everyone else. But to make this book more readable, the male pronouns *he* or *his* will be used to refer to individuals of unspecified gender rather than the clunkier *he/she* or *his/hers.* It is not my intention to offend anyone.

INTRODUCTION

When was the last time you escaped a massacre, rampage, or spree shooting? For most of us, the answer is never—thank goodness. The good news is that these events are relatively few and far between. The bad news is they are becoming more common, and you only have to experience one. The places where such killings have occurred include schools, colleges, offices, factories, courthouses, hospitals, churches, nursing homes, malls, and even military bases. They have taken place in rural areas, the suburbs, and big cities all across America. But killing sprees aren't uniquely American, despite what those in the media might imply. They occur in many countries, including Great Britain, Finland, Japan, India, Spain, and Germany. In short, they happen everywhere.

This book is not intended to be the answer to every possible mass-killing scenario, nor is it intended to be a history of previous rampage shootings. We can learn a lot from looking at previous events, and in Part One I analyze examples of rampages in school and other public settings. This helps put what we are likely to see in the future in perspective, while at the same time providing suggestions for avoiding or dealing with other types of criminal acts. Primarily, this book is intended to get people to think about violent situations and explore different courses of action that might allow them to either avoid or survive them. Part Two discuss various strategies and tactics for doing so.

What I have attempted to do with this book is to examine incidents of spree killings, listen to what the "experts" are saying, and add my own carefully thought out ideas and suggestions. The following quote aptly expresses my view on the importance of research:

> "Research is to see what everyone else has seen and think what no one else has thought."
> —Albert Szent-Györgyi,
> Nobel Prize for Physiology or Medicine,
> 1937

OK, you know that spree killings are a national (and international) epidemic—is there anything *you* do? This book focuses on what the average person can do to survive the first deadly minutes of these events. One of the problems that makes rampages so unique is that they are often over before trained law enforcement professionals can arrive at the scene. This places the burden on the people caught in the rampage to do the right things and take care of themselves. This book will provide motivated individuals with tactics and strategies to improve their odds of staying alive.

This book will show you how to recognize the early signs of an incipient attack so that you can prevent or avoid it or, failing that, survive it. Knowing the who, what, and why could mean the difference between life and death—for you and others for whom you may be responsible. The why is an important consideration because it can affect the success of any strategy you devise. Are you the intended target, or are you collateral damage? If you are not the target, the shooter will be less concerned about where you go or what you are doing. If you are the target, getting away is more difficult. Chapters 2 and 3 examine actual spree killings in public places and in schools to see how these factors apply.

As anyone involved in dealing with life-and-death situations on

Introduction

a regular basis can tell you, training until it becomes second nature is critical if you are to survive any assault. This is especially so with spree killings, which are explosive and provide little or no time to think. Your response must be initiated in milliseconds. Anyone who thinks he can come up with a viable plan without having trained for the situation is delusional. Knowing what it takes to survive, and incorporating those components into your plan of action, is the subject of Chapter 5.

Most rampage killers are motivated by similar urges as anyone else, such as revenge, hate, being disrespected or ridiculed, or extreme fear of others. The difference is that they act on these feelings. The number-one survival technique is to learn to recognize the signs of bizarre, erratic, or suspicious behavior, and to take proactive steps. Chapter 6 shows you how to remain alert so that you recognize the first signs of danger—in time to take preventive action.

So, can you survive a rampage shooting? The answer is that most people do. Some people survive by luck, and some survive by executing an effective strategy. I will accept luck, but I don't like to rely on it because sooner or later it runs out. I am more concerned with doing things that improve my odds.

Of course, it is important to acknowledge the 100-percent rule: nothing works 100 percent of the time. No plan, strategy, or technique is infallible. So a strategy that worked in one incident might not work in another. Backup plans are essential, but when training time is limited, often a simple one-size-fits-all response gets programmed in (lockdowns in schools are a classic example). Such a generic response can lead to disaster. That's why I emphasize the importance of realistic training throughout this book and especially in my suggestions for educators and law enforcement agencies in Chapters 8 and 9.

For many years, I have made it my business to review the hundreds of articles on shooting incidents and attacks in schools and public places. By carefully reading these accounts, I was able to extract information that I believe could be useful in preventing or surviving future incidents. In some cases, I noted the perpetrators' methods. In other cases, I highlighted patterns that emerged from similar attacks. I tried to determine if the survivors did something tactical that helped them survive or just lucked out, or vice versa for those who didn't make it. Let me be the first to acknowledge: luck often plays a major part in who survives these killings.

Your assignment after reading this book is to study any accounts you can get your hands on about any spree killings to see what steps the victims and survivors took. In many cases, this information might be sketchy, so you will have to do the best you can.

When I was still teaching school, students often advised me, "I have to learn from my own mistakes." My answer to them was "I prefer to learn from the mistakes of others." In the case of deadly rampages, learning from your own mistakes might cost you your life. In life-or-death-situations, it is imperative that we learn from the actions and mistakes of others.

PART I

DEFINING THE PROBLEM

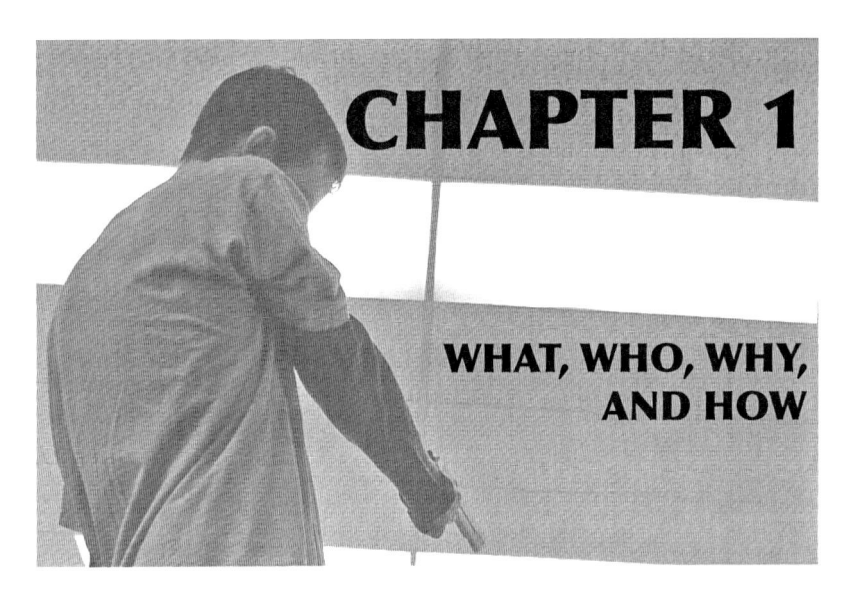

CHAPTER 1

WHAT, WHO, WHY, AND HOW

Definitions can be interesting. A *spree killing* occurs at two or more locations with almost no time break between the murders. A *mass murder* typically takes place at one location. Those in law enforcement currently favor the term *active shooter*, as opposed to *spree killer* or *rampage killer,* when describing ongoing shootings.

While each of the above has a slightly different definition according to the law enforcement community, I favor the term *spree killing* or *rampage killing* instead of *spree shooting* or *rampage shooting* because shooting is just one of the many options open to these killers. The narrow definition of a shooter would limit the scope and usefulness of this work. But I have used all these terms somewhat interchangeably throughout this book.

WHAT

Whatever term you wish to use for these killings, sadly there are far too many recent examples of them, and there is no doubt in my mind that they will continue. These days, massacres seem to be a regular occurrence somewhere in the world. At a news conference after a shooting at Long Beach Memorial Medical Center, local Police Chief Batts noted, "This is becoming a national trend." I second that but hasten to add that it is also becoming an international trend.

Despite the impression of some, killing rampages don't just happen in the United States. In fact, they are far more common worldwide than in the United States. After careful consideration, I elected to include examples of international killing sprees in this book. Several factors influenced my decision. First, because of air travel, global media, and porous borders, America is no longer the isolated safe haven it once was. Therefore, world events can easily influence domestic events, and vice versa. Second, international attacks can easily be an indicator of things to come here. These killers often research past events, using tactics that worked and eliminating those that didn't. It is important for us to learn from international events so that we can prevent them from happening here or at least be on guard. Lastly, Americans are frequent travelers abroad. Terrorists often target foreigners, and Americans are highly valued as targets. The survival tactics and strategies discussed in this book are portable—don't leave home without them.

Links Between Various Forms of Violence

What many people fail to realize is that there is often a connection between various forms of violence. If you don't understand the connections, it is like sticking your finger in a dike to stop the flow of water. In rampage shootings, we often see a link to emotional or mental instability, bullying, revenge, and suicide.

It is often impossible to separate one form of violence from another, and on occasion we see one form of violence flow into another. A spree shooting can easily trigger a panic riot. Now in addition to being shot, there is the risk of being crushed or trampled by an out-of-control mob. Likewise, a hostage scenario can easily turn into a massacre. Each of the following attacks—Beslan School massacre (Soviet Union, 2004), Lima, Peru, embassy hostage scenario (1996), and the Columbine High School massacre (Littleton, Colorado, April 20, 1999)—involved hundreds or even thousands of innocent bystanders, and each at times had elements of a hostage scenario, panic rioting, and massacre. The Binghamton, New York, spree shooting (April 2009), which left 14 dead (including the shooter) and 24 wounded, also had hostages trapped in various parts of the building and widespread panic during the initial shooting spree.

WHO

When we examine the background and history of a spree shooter in depth, we can often easily see why he did what he did. However, the problem is that we can't necessarily predict who will become a shooter. It appears that most mass killers exhibit certain red flags, or danger signs, but these are often not obvious before the shooting. In addition, the criminal justice system doesn't allow us to arrest someone for what he might do. After all, there are many people out there with red flags flying who don't become mass murderers. So predicting who will become a mass killer is far from a perfect science.

The one definite thing we know about all spree killers is that they aren't all alike. They range in age from 11 (Andrew Golden, one of the killers at Westside Middle School, outside Jonesboro, Arkansas) to 88 (James Wenneker von Brunn, the shooter at the U.S. Holocaust Memorial Museum in Washington, D.C.). Though most are white, some spree killers have been black, Asian, Hispanic, and Native American. A few spree killers have been female, though this is rare.

Motivations vary, though most are driven by revenge or a perceived grievance, either real or imaginary. Most (but not all) of these killers can be classified as emotionally disturbed—though this is sometimes not recognized until after the killings. Some shooters have specific targets; others don't. Some are angry at society at large and target indiscriminately. Some act alone (e.g., Cho at Virginia Tech) whereas others plot their deadly acts with one or more like-minded souls (e.g., the Columbine killers).

Spree killers seldom act impulsively. Instead, they nurse their grievances and carefully plan their revenge, some for a long time. The Columbine duo plotted their attack for more than a year. The killers plan their attack, gather weapons and supplies, train, and practice. Doing all this requires effort, which may well alter the person's activities, schedule, demeanor, or attitude. These changes may tip off family, friends, coworkers, or classmates that the person is up to something, who in turn can notify the police. The likelihood of detecting such intentions beforehand improves dramatically if observers are trained to see early warning signs of violence.

The following story epitomizes what society is facing. On September 23, 2008, Matti Saari, 22, walked into the Kauhajoki School of Hospitality (in western Finland), where he was a second-year culinary arts student, and shot and killed 10 people before shooting himself. He died a few hours later. The tragic thing is that about a year before the murders Saari had posted chilling footage of himself on YouTube, which alarmed police enough to bring him in for questioning. Police let him go because they did not have enough evidence to charge him with anything or take away his weapon (he had a temporary permit for it). On the Friday before the shootings, Saari posted new footage of himself on a social networking site, firing a handgun and saying, "You will die next." Police did not see this clip before Saari killed his victims; it they had, the tragedy might have been prevented. (*Newsday,* September, 24, 2008.)

The Suicide-Homicide Link

The FBI suggests that there is a fine line between suicide and homicide. The determining factor is whether the anger is directed inward (suicide) or outward (homicide). It is important to keep in mind this link when dealing with suicidal people who show signs of violence because they could pose a very serious threat to the public. Punishment is not a deterrent to them.

Most rampage killers have no plans to escape (an exception to this were the Westside Middle School shooters, who packed their van with camping gear and supplies). Instead, suicide is their end plan, either by their own hand or by that of a cop. As evidence of this, there are two things that mass killers *almost* never do. First, most don't wear a ballistic vest during the attack, even though these are both legal and easy to come by. In fact, I could find only one example where a spree shooter had a Kevlar vest: Jiverly Voong who shot up the American Civic Center in Binghamton, New York, in 2009. Second, most mass killers don't make an attempt to fortify a position from which to engage police. The two exceptions to the second point are the Amish school and Virginia Tech killers.

The Racist/Hater

The Internet provides an excellent opportunity for a racist or hater to focus his ideas. Dr. Kathleen Blee, a sociologist professor and department chair at the University of Pittsburgh, says, "What the Internet does is get people to focus, to make their racist and violent ideas much more coherent and much more targeted toward particular kinds of people. They [racist websites] give people a sense that violence is not only possible for somebody to commit, but laudatory" (*Southern Poverty Law Center Intelligence Report*, Summer 2009).

Dr. Randy Blazak, author of the book *Renegade Kids, Suburban Outlaws: From Youth Culture to Delinquency*, concurs: "The danger is in people who are already predisposed to racial violence. They may find the validation and justification for criminal behavior within an online peer group."

Many, but not all, of these haters can be classified as sociopaths or persons with antisocial personality disorder. These people are encouraged by the Internet to do horrific things and to feel justified in doing them. Dr. Elizabeth Englander, director of the Massachusetts Aggression Reduction Center at Bridgewater State College, Massachusetts, notes, "If you have a severe mental illness that leads to delusions, then you could read something on the Internet and say, 'That was written to me individually. It's a secret message,'" (*Southern Poverty Law Center Intelligence Report*, Summer 2009).

The Lone Wolf

A lone wolf is a person operating alone without direct affiliation to a specific group. Racism or some other type of hatred is also often a factor in lone-wolf attacks. The following is an example of a murderous rampage by a lone wolf who was inspired by propaganda on the Internet.

On January 21, 2009, 22-year-old Keith Luke, a self-described white supremacist, set out on a crime spree in Brockton, Massachusetts, to kill as many "nonwhites" as he could. He shot and murdered two black immigrants and sexually assaulted and attempted to murder a third. Then he headed for the local synagogue, where he intended to shoot Jews as they left their weekly bingo game. He then planned to kill himself. Police intercepted and arrested him before he got to the synagogue. Luke told police investigators that he had spent hours online trolling white supremacist websites and often left remarks on the message boards. While awaiting trial, Luke carved a swastika on his forehead, Charles Manson–style. *(Southern Poverty Law Center Report*, Spring 2009.)

Lone-wolf killing sprees often involve a great deal of collateral damage to others as the killers try to target a specific person, organization, or location. Timothy McVeigh's murderous spree at the federal center in Oklahoma City is a classic example (though McVeigh did have an accomplice, Terry Nichols) as are abortion clinic bombings.

Attacks by lone wolves are among the hardest to prevent. They can be planned secretly and without much or any intergroup communication. These attacks can occur anywhere, and often no clues are available beforehand. In some cases, an observant teacher or student has found evidence in the notebook of a student that linked him to a violent group, which allowed school administrators or law enforcement to step in and prevent a planned killing spree.

The Fragile Person

A fragile person doesn't get along well with others and will probably take any correction as an insult or as being picked on. Many victims of bullies may perceive that everyone is victimizing them. A social "pecking order" is at work in every group. Those at the bottom often feel they are being bullied, even though their treatment doesn't really meet the definition of bullying and others in the group fail to see this as bullying or any type of negative treatment. However, when it comes to perception versus reality, it is perception that counts. If someone feels he is a victim, then that is his reality. The problems in dealing with extremely sensitive or fragile people are (1) they often hide their perceptions, and (2) it is hard to know when or if they will go over the edge.

A case in point is Michael McLendon, who was responsible for the worst spree shooting in Alabama history on March 10, 2009. McLendon's killing spree spanned two counties in rural Alabama and left 11 people dead, including six members of his family, two neighbors, and the gunman himself. In examining this case, we find that the 28-year-old gunman struggled to keep a job and left behind a list of employers and coworkers he believed had wronged him. It was interesting, however, he did not retaliate against the former employers. Instead, he went after his family and what appeared to be strangers. In McLendon's home, investigators found a hit list that contained the names of several local corporations and a letter from him admitting that he had killed his mother and he planned to commit suicide.

With the numbers of people losing their jobs, past experience has clearly shown this will increase the number of rampage killings. In addition, a record number of federal job discrimination complaints filed have been filed in the past couple of years (*Newsday*, March 12, 2009). Both of these factors indicate that there could be more acts of retaliation by emotionally disturbed people.

The Gang Member

No community or school is safe from the spectre of gangs. There are a multitude of gangs, and membership can be based on race or ethnicity, neighborhoods, criminal activities, and other factors. Usually, where you have gangs, you have violence, which can be motivated by acquiring a reputation, seeking revenge for an act or sign of disrespect, or passing an initiation. Occasionally, this violence takes the form of spree killings. Many gang members are involved in criminal activities, especially drugs sales, and do not seem to be bothered by killing competitors or innocent bystanders. Drive-by shootings are common in gangs; these shootings may target specific individuals or rival gangs, or be completely random.

A frightening new twist is that gang members are joining the U.S. military. Looking at photos of sections of Iraq, it is surprising to see gang graffiti from many different gangs on the buildings and walls. One estimate is that there are as many as 10,000 street gang members currently serving in the military. The importance of this is that when they leave the military they share their military skills (e.g., marksmanship, explosives, demolitions) with fellow gang members. Additionally, the organizational skills taught in the military can be used to make gangs more proficient. Recent gang shootings have reflected some of this military training. Law enforcement professionals are noting how this military training is transforming gangs into more efficient "killing machines."

Mexican drug violence, which threatens the peace and tranquility in Mexico, has spread across the border into the United States. Most of the killings in Mexico have been gang on gang, but there are always innocent victims who get in the way. U.S. border towns, which are transit points for drugs smuggled in from Mexico, have been experiencing increased violence. In late January 2010, in Ciudad Juarez, which is just across the border from El Paso, Texas, 16 people were killed by armed men who arrived in trucks, blocked off the streets, and began killing. Among the victims were 10 students, aged 13–19 who were attending a birthday party. Several more people were seriously injured. The police theorized that the shooting was sparked by a dispute over drug territory, but none of the teenagers were involved in the drug trade.

Phoenix has now achieved the dubious distinction of being the number-two city in the world for kidnappings. Currently, it is gang-on-gang kidnapping and murder, but who knows when that could spread to the general population and become spree killings?

What, Who, Why, and How

WHY

Obviously, there is a close connection between the who and the why, and you will see that link in all the examples cited in this book. Why killers kill is a complicated subject, and space prohibits me from delving into it very deeply in this book. If you are interested, there are a number of serious studies that attempt to answer this question. Check the bibliography in the back of this book for some of the titles I consulted.

Mental Health

The reasons for spree killings vary from situation to situation. The most common reasons are revenge and mental illness, which often goes undiagnosed until after the killings. In the past, killers have been set off by bullying, hatred, loss of a job or relationship, or depression. I discuss the issue of mental illness in more depth in Chapter 3, "Spree Killings in Schools," because symptoms of mental illness usually first appear in children (sometimes as early as elementary school) and can be treated more successfully when they first appear.

Economic Influences

In the past, every downturn in the economy has resulted in an increase in crime and violence, including bank robberies, assaults, and murders. So far, this new dip in the economy is living up to the worst expectations. With the increasing numbers of layoffs, business failures, and foreclosures, we are bound to see an increase in spree killings. In looking over past killings involving adults, unemployment is a significant factor in a number of the cases. Sometimes the killers target former employers or coworkers, and sometimes random crowds at malls, offices, or public arenas.

Media Influence

Print media, TV, Internet, and other media outlets have a tremendous influence over people. Just look at what happens after any shooting or bomb threat that gets media attention: copycats come out of the woodwork with threats. Calling in a bomb threat allows a prankster or powerless person to feel powerful. Every year on the anniversary of the Columbine shooting, schools around the country receive numerous threats, resulting in thousands of evacuations. In July 2007 two teens at Connectquot High School in Bohemia, New York, were charged with plotting a Columbine-like attack on their school on the eighth anniversary of the Columbine attack. Even though the "experts" say that 99.9 percent of threats called in are false, school officials cannot take the chance of not acting on such a threat. Searching most school buildings is a monumental job, taking a day at least with sufficient manpower and dogs. How can officials be expected to do a thorough job in under an hour?

In particular, the Internet has added a whole new dimension to spreading threats and rumors, as well as disseminating information on how to carry out violent acts. It can also bring together people with like interests. Regardless of how extreme, bizarre, or detestable a person's actions might be, there are those out there who encourage them. Pedophiles use the Internet as a meeting place and an opportunity to exchange ideas. Racist and hate groups use websites quite effectively to spread their ideas and recruit members. We have seen how these sometimes inspire spree killers. Young people worldwide use the Internet to express their reverence for the Columbine killers, as well as their plans to top their horrendous act. Police are constantly uncovering new plots that Harris and Klebold have inspired posthumously.

Video Game Connection

Can video games lead to spree shootings? This is a hotly debated topic, but many believe they already have. Since 1996, at least 11 mass murderers showed an excessive interest in playing violent video games. The problem is, millions of other people play the same games and don't become killers. Around the world, pilots, soldiers, and law enforcement people not only recognize the value of video simulators, but also train their people with them. Why? Because they work.

What, Who, Why, and How

However, training professionals with simulators has one big difference: these men have control and discipline working for them. Sadly, many of the people watching these games don't. Even more frightening, these simulators can improve the viewer's combat ability.

An avid video game player, Kimveer Gill shot 19 people at Dawson College in Canada before killing himself. On his website, the 19-year-old student had posted that he enjoyed playing *Postal* and *Super Columbine Massacre*. Can you imagine video game titles like these? Fortunately for everyone, Kimveer was not a great shot. He killed only one person, but not for a lack of trying, before committing suicide.

Tribal Influence

Man has an innate need to be part of a community. Prehistoric man belonged to a tribe for safety reasons. Each tribe established its own territory to ensure ample food supplies and protected that territory from other groups. This survival mechanism has carried over to today. Many of the conflicts around the world are caused by tribal, ethnic, or clan conflicts. The need to belong is powerful and is one reason given for the growth of gangs all across the country.

Students join groups in school: teams, fraternities or sororities, clubs, or cliques. Adults also tend to associate in groups, whether formal or informal. Groups tend to be exclusive, and so some people are left out. Many then go off and form their own groups; others don't or can't for a variety or reasons (e.g., poor social skills, money, race, or ethnicity). Those who can't find a group to fit into are often designated as losers or loners. Plus, as in the caste system in India, not all groups possess the same status in society. Over time, the negativity of being at the lowest level can take its toll on individuals who are unable to move up. Those at the bottom of the pecking order are often easy marks for bullies, which makes for an explosive situation. And these feelings of resentment or alienation can explode in a rampage. This problem exists in every country, town, school, corporation, and organization.

As I explained, serial killers were excluded from this study because they are not by definition spree killers, but I think that the information below also applies to some spree killers as well. In his work on serial killers, Dr. Michael Stone concluded that three critical factors were present in all the serial killers he investigated: mental illness, brain damage, and child abuse (sexual, physical, or mental, or a combination). When the first two are present, this third factor seems to be the spark that lights the fuse. Although many with severe mental illness are not necessarily violent or dangerous, when it is present with brain damage and abuse, you have a monster in the making. This monster could be a serial murderer or a spree killer, depending on a number of factors. (Discovery Channel, August 17, 2006.)

HOW

How the attack is carried out is often determined by who the killer is. Is the killer out for revenge against a targeted few or against anyone in his path? If he is after revenge against a specific person or place (e.g., school, workplace, family, or wife), the person will take targeted action. If he is angry with the world in general, then he might select a soft target to provide him the largest body count possible.

Planned or Spontaneous?

Are most spree killings spur of the moment, or do they show careful and lengthy planning? (By spur of the moment, I mean within the same day.) Both occur, but most rampages are planned, as it takes time to get the weapons and other equipment assembled. For example, a number of indicators point toward deliberation in the Virginia Tech rampage. Cho created an extensive amount of material justifying his shooting and sent it to the news media between his two attacks.

Weapons

Since guns are readily available, glamorized in the media, and effective at instilling fear, they are the most common choice of spree killers in the United States. They can include handguns, assault rifles, and shotguns. Guns can inflict damage from a distance, making it more difficult for someone to get close enough to disarm the killer. Guns also give a sense of power to the shooter.

It is worth noting, however, that spree killers have used a variety of other weapons in place of (or in conjunction with) guns. Around the world, bombs seem to be quite popular, especially with terrorists. A culture where edged weapons play an important role and are readily accessible increases the likelihood that blades will be the weapon of choice. In Africa, over the years there have been numerous machete and knife attacks generated out of hate and revenge, many of which were tribally motivated. Japan has experienced a number of rampage knife assaults.

Even here in the United States, you may be shocked to learn that edged weapons are the second leading cause of homicides, behind handguns, and that they kill more people than rifles and shotguns combined (*FBI Law Enforcement Bulletin*, April 2009). After a focused effort by law enforcement to get guns off the street in certain areas of New York City, police saw knives and other sharp objects emerge as the weapons of choice in many killings in 2008. Gun murders in the city dropped from 347 in 2007 to 292 in 2008, but there was a 50-percent increase in edged-weapon murders (*Newsday*, July 7, 2009).

The deadliest school attack in the United States occurred in 1927 in Bath Township, Michigan, and no gun was involved (*Law and Order,* June 2009). A disgruntled school board member, upset over an increase in school taxes, placed dynamite charges around the Bath school building, which resulted in 45 people dead and at least 58 injured (mostly children). A secondary explosion that targeted responders killed several more, including the bomber.

Spree killers will often bring along multiple weapons. The Columbine killers, Eric Harris and Dylan Klebold, intended to do maximum damage and brought along 30 pipe bombs and two propane tanks. The propane tanks had detonation timers and were set to go off in the cafeteria during a crowded lunch period. The two then planned to shoot students as they fled the lunchroom. Fortunately, the timers malfunctioned, and the pipe bombs were never used, or the death toll would have been much higher than the 13 killed and 21 injured. We cannot always count on the killers' ineptitude.

Another example of a killer using multiple weapons is the Luby Cafeteria attack in Killeen, Texas (October 16, 1991), which began with George Hennard smashing his pickup truck through the front window of the restaurant. The attacker then began shooting people, killing 23 and injuring another 20. This was the deadliest massacre in U.S. history until Virginia Tech.

Yet another example of an attacker using multiple weapons—none of them a firearm—occurred in Ansbach, Germany, on September 17, 2009. Armed with three Molotov cocktails, an ax, and two knives, an unnamed 18-year-old male wounded eight students and a teacher at his high school before being shot and arrested by police. The teen had no criminal record, and his motive was unknown.

Are Firearms a Red Flag?

In rural communities firearms are very common. Many people train in the use of firearms for professional or recreational purposes, are members of shooting clubs, or practice at public ranges, and they are not dangerous people. However, when a sudden interest in firearms is combined with other signs of trouble—such as poor behavior in school, fighting, excessive absences from school or work, obsession with violent video games, or verbal or written threats—this is a definite red flag.

Before the Dunblane, Scotland, massacre in 1996, which claimed the lives of 16 primary school children and one adult, Thomas Hamilton could often be found at a shooting club or public range. Robert Steinhauser, who killed 16 people at his prep school in Erfurt, Germany, in 2002, joined shooting clubs so that he could develop his shooting skills and gain access to weapons and ammunition. Thirteen-year-old Mitchell Johnson and 11-year-old Andrew Golden killed five and wounded 10 in a carefully designed sniper attack on their middle school outside Jonesboro, Arkansas, in 1998. Golden was given a gun at age 6 and later began practicing at a gun club, likely with his parents' approval. Johnson learned to shoot from his mother and was later sent to a three-week course to improve his skills.

In most of the active-shooter scenarios, the shooter had multiple weapons and lots of ammo. Charles Whitman, the sniper who killed 14 from the bell tower at the University of Texas in 1966—widely regarded as the person who brought the term *spree killer* into the American lexicon—had military training. He stockpiled ammunition, weapons, and military equipment, as have several other spree killers. Whitman had 700 rounds with him. Charles Roberts, who attacked the Amish schoolhouse in Pennsylvania in 2006, had 600 rounds of ammo with him. Matthew Murray, who attempted to commit mass murder in a church in Colorado, took 1,000 rounds of ammo with him. Ammunition has a long shelf life, so those planning a killing spree can acquire guns and ammo over a long period, which draws less attention than making a single large purchase. While stockpiling firearms and ammunition alone might not indicate a threat, it could focus attention on other threat assessment factors that signal the potential for violence.

A number of shooters combined other tactics with firearms for their deadly assaults. Charles Roberts used cable ties in the Amish school attack. In the Colorado Springs church attack, Matthew Murray brought smoke-generating devices, which fortunately did not go off. In addition to his firearms, the Virginia Tech shooter also brought along chains to lock the doors before entering the engineering building, which both prevented students from escaping and delayed the entrance of police officers.

Killing Family Members

As mentioned earlier, this is not a study of family annihilators, but there is sometimes a connection between killing family members and killing others. At least a half dozen of the spree shootings discussed in this book were preceded by the murder of family members. Charles

Surviving a Massacre, Rampage, or Spree Killing

Whitman (University of Texas, 1966), Luke Woodham (Pearl High School, Pearl, Mississippi, 1997), Kip Kinkle (Thurston High School, Springfield, Oregon, 1998), Mark Barton (Atlanta, Georgia, trading firms, 1999), Jeff Weise (Red Lake Senior High, Red Lake, Minnesota, 2005), and Michael McLendon (Alabama, 2009) all killed family members before starting their killing rampages. Family annihilators, on the other hand, usually kill only family members and then themselves.

CONCLUSION

There are many factors that could result in someone becoming a mass murderer. With the wide variety of potential violent offenders out there, it is not surprising that there are deadly rampages almost daily. The real question is whether there are ways of reducing some of the factors that lead to these killings.

I have repeatedly emphasized the need to identify mental health problems early, which might prevent future violence and reduce the number of people who are incarcerated. Little kids equal little problems; big kids equal big problems. As problems fester, they get worse. The jails are full of people with mental health problems. The cost of incarceration is astronomical, averaging around $25,000 per person annually. Could counseling services provided in elementary school prevent some of these criminal careers? I would like to think so, but at least we owe our children the chance to straighten out.

Currently, society appears to be more reactive than proactive. Until we get more thoughtful leadership, I don't see the situation improving. That being said, this places the burden of personal safety on the individual. Being alert is one of the most effective ways you can protect yourself or your loved ones. Part II will show you some strategies and techniques for recognizing the danger signs of a rampage.

CHAPTER 2

SPREE KILLINGS IN PUBLIC PLACES

There are two inherent risks when you are in large groups. First, spree killers target large groups for obvious reasons: lots of people = lots of victims. Favorite targets include schools, airports, office parks, churches, and mass transit sites, among others. In addition to offering multiple targets, crowds make it difficult for people to escape.

Second, when large groups panic, there is a greater chance of being crushed or trampled. For this reason, experts recommend that you stay on the periphery whenever possible in the presence of large groups. It is also important to be aware of and close to an exit or escape route. This is more important when the group is in an enclosed area, such as a stadium, concert hall, or restaurant.

On the other hand, being in a large group can also make you safer in certain situations. As one of many, the statistical chance of your being the target of a random attack is diminished. Also being in the center of a large group reduces the risk of an attacker from the outside getting to you. However, these risks pale in comparison to the danger of being crushed or trampled by a panicking mob.

The following stories are just a handful of examples of killings in public places (schools are covered in the next chapter).

Surviving a Massacre, Rampage, or Spree Killing

MARKETS AND MALLS

An attack at a mall or marketplace could start for any number of reasons. A disgruntled customer or employee seeking revenge, or an argument between shoppers that escalates into something bigger could spark it. Here are some examples of deadly attacks in malls or market settings in recent years:

- On April 2, 2009, Jiverly Voong, 42, carried a high-powered rifle, two handguns, and a satchel of ammunition into the American Civic Center in Binghamton, New York. He killed 13, seriously wounded five, and then committed suicide. Before entering the building, he used his car to barricade the back door of the building to prevent anyone from escaping. Voong was wearing a bulletproof vest, which is unusual for spree shooters, especially those who intend to kill themselves.

  Two dozen people barricaded themselves in the boiler room, which turned out to be a smart move. The receptionist was shot as Voong came in the front door, but she survived by playing dead and hiding for 40 minutes until police arrived. The receptionist had made the initial 911 call, and police were on the scene in three or four minutes but didn't enter the building for more than 30 minutes.

  Voong was no stranger to the American Civic Center; he had studied English there before dropping out a month before the shootings. Two possible reasons were given for the rampage: Voong had recently been laid off, and apparently he was quite upset that people made fun of his poor English, which he saw as a sign of disrespect.

- On Sunday, June 8, 2008, in the popular electronics and video game district of Akihabara, in central Tokyo, a man first plowed into a crowd with his truck and then got out and began stabbing people in the confusion. In all he stabbed 17 people (including a policeman), killing seven. The Akihabara massacre occurred on the seventh anniversary of a mass stabbing at a Japanese elementary school. Was there a connection, or was it a coincidence? The 25-year-old told police that he was "tired of life and sick of everything," and that he came there to kill people. According to a witness, the suspect dropped the knife after police threatened to shoot him, and he was arrested.

- On December 4, 2007, Robert A. Hawkins, 19, opened fire in a busy mall department store in Omaha, Nebraska, killing nine before committing suicide. An hour before the shootings, his mother found a suicide note and contacted the sheriff's department. The note indicated that he intended an act that would make him "famous" but didn't give specifics. Hawkins had been under psychiatric care since age 6, and at the time of the shootings was estranged from his family and living with friends. They described him as "troubled." He dropped out of high school in his senior year. He was reportedly upset over being fired from his job and breaking up with his girlfriend. Police arrived six minutes after the initial 911 call.

- On April 30, 2007, David Logdon, 51, shot and killed two people in the parking lot outside a Target store in Center Mall, one of the busiest shopping centers in the Kansas City area. While en route to the mall, Logdon had been stopped by a police officer because he was driving a stolen car (the car's owner, Logdon's neighbor, had been found dead in her home), but he shot the officer in the arm and fled. But police were able to track the stolen car to the mall and arrived at the mall much more quickly than if they had been called after the shootings in the parking lot. Logdon was killed by a police officer when he went inside the mall. Logdon was said to be upset because his application for a private security license was denied. His family described him as mentally ill and suicidal.

Surviving a Massacre, Rampage, or Spree Killing

- On February 12, 2007, at the Trolley Square Mall in Salt Lake City, Utah, Salamin Talbit (also spelled Sulejman Talovic), 18, wearing a trench coat and carrying a 12-gauge shotgun and a pistol, calmly started shooting people. He killed four before an off-duty police officer shot and killed him. Initially, many shoppers thought the shots were balloons bursting and didn't respond. (By paying closer attention to your surroundings, you might be aware of danger before it is too late to escape or take action.) Talbit had relocated to the United States with his family from Bosnia and Herzegovina when he was 10. His family and police offered no motive for the murders. He had minor run-ins with the law and liked to hang out at the mall.

- On February 13, 2005, Robert Bonelli Jr., 24, emptied an assault rifle inside a store in the Hudson Valley Mall in Upstate New York, near Glasco. Interestingly, either Bonelli never intended to kill anyone or he was the worst shot imaginable. He reportedly fired 60 rounds into a crowd estimated at around 3,000 people, injuring three, none fatally. When he ran out of ammunition, a couple of shoppers restrained him until police arrived. When police searched his home, they found an altar to the Columbine shooters and videos of Bonelli exploding homemade pipe bombs.

- On August 19, 1987, Michael Ryan, 27, killed 16 people in the small market town of Hungerford, England, with a Kalashnikov rifle. He killed himself after being cornered by police. Ryan was reported to be fascinated with firearms, and he was unemployed at the time of the spree. The British government responded to the massacre with a ban on semiautomatic rifles.

PUBLIC TRANSPORTATION SITES

Public transportation seems to be a popular spot for attacks, especially for terrorists: about 30 percent of terrorist attacks worldwide

Spree Killings in Public Places

have targeted public transportation (*FBI Law Enforcement Bulletin*, July 2009). One analysis studied more than 22,000 terrorist attacks between 1968 and 2004, and found that of all targets, mass transit sites had the highest casualty rates. Public transportation venues are crowded much of the time and offer lots of soft targets to pick from.

In addition to the high casualty rates, damage to public transport could easily disrupt transportation schedules, damage the local economy, and destroy public trust in government, a main goal of terrorism. In spite of improved security, new surveillance systems, and enhanced regulations regarding explosives, American public transportation sites remain vulnerable, according to most experts, who view these targets as too attractive for international and domestic terrorists to pass up.

Below are a few incidents of sprees at public transportation sites, including several with terrorist connections. I offer these (even though I excluded terrorism in general from this book) because of the lessons that can be taken from them and applied to spree killings.

- The Mumbai terrorist attack in Mumbai, India (November 26–29, 2008), also included killings at the railway terminal. Reports from an eyewitness claimed that the police hid to avoid engaging the armed terrorist as he walked down the platform firing an assault rifle. During the attack on the city, at least 173 were reported dead and more than 300 injured.

- On July 7, 2005, a group of Islamic extremists attacked a number of transportation lines of the London Underground, detonating bombs on several underground trains. Four suicide bombers were involved, and 52 people were killed and more than 700 injured. Two weeks later, on July 21, 2005, another series of four bombing attacks on London's transport system occurred. Fortunately, the main explosives on these four bombs in the second attack failed to detonate, and there were no casualties.

Surviving a Massacre, Rampage, or Spree Killing

- In March 2004, al-Qaeda assisted terrorists bombed the Madrid, Spain, train station, killing 191 people. According to law enforcement sources, the attack cost $50,000 to accomplish and was financed through drug sales. This bombing, just before elections in Spain, resulted in Spain withdrawing its troops from Iraq. Does terrorism work? Don't think the terrorists haven't learned an important lesson from this.

- On December 5, 2003, a train bombing in Stavropol, Russia, killed 41 and injured 150. Chechen rebels were suspected. Chechen terrorists were also suspected in the suicide bombing at a Moscow metro station a couple of months later on February 6, 2004, killing 41 and injuring 230.

- March 20,1995, domestic Japanese terrorists used sarin gas to attack a Tokyo subway, killing 12 and injuring more than 5,000. Four suspects were found guilty.

- On December 7, 1993, Colin Ferguson, 35, boarded a Long Island commuter train in New York and, apparently angry at the world and everyone in it, decided to take out his anger on passengers, all strangers, on their way home. Carrying a 9mm Ruger pistol and 160 rounds, Ferguson started at the back of the car and fired two magazines into standing passengers and those who had fallen to the ground. He killed six and wounded 19 before finally being stopped by three passengers who tackled him to the ground.

    Ferguson, who was clearly emotionally disturbed (if not mentally ill), refused an attorney and decided to represent himself in court. On February 17, 1995, Ferguson was convicted of six consecutive life sentences. What made this case unusual was that Ferguson is one of the few black spree killers on record. Born in Jamaica, he was the son of one of the wealthiest and most prominent businessmen in Jamaica. Ferguson was a good student, graduating third in his class in Kingston. Both his parents died when he was 20, and their deaths deeply disturbed him, as well as having wiped out the family's wealth. Ferguson immigrated to New York, and his situation steadily deteriorated. He was distressed by what he saw as racism directed toward him and his inability to find a job befitting him. His behavior was marked by bouts of aggression, which cost him several jobs and his marriage and got him expelled from a class he was taking. He began openly advocating violence toward whites. Those who had contact with him described him as dangerous and mentally unstable.

PARADES, CONCERTS, AND SPORTING EVENTS

Another favorite venue for mass murderers is a parade, concert, or sporting event, where again you have a lot of people squeezed into a small space with limited exits. The following are examples of killings at such events.

- On April 30, 2009, Karst Tates, 38, deliberately drove his car through police barricades in an attempt to ram an open-topped bus carrying members of the Dutch royal family during the Dutch Queen's Day Parade in Apeldoorn, Netherlands. Eight people died from injuries they received as they were run over by the car. Tates also later died of injuries received during the attack.

- On Fat Tuesday, February 25, 2009, two men, 18 and 19, opened fire on the crowd during a Mardi Gras parade in New Orleans. The parade turned chaotic when people started ducking and running in all directions. No one was killed, but seven people were struck, including a toddler. Police apprehended the two gunmen at the scene and booked them on seven counts of attempted first-degree murder. The shots were apparently random.

- On December 9, 2004, shooter Nathan Gale, 25, rushed the stage at a Columbus, Ohio, concert by heavy-metal band Damageplan, shooting and killing the band's guitarist, Darrell "Dimebag" Abbott. Gale shot Darrell five times, including once in the head, and then began shooting at the audience, killing three more and injuring seven. The shooter reloaded at least once. When a police officer arrived, Gale was holding a man hostage in a headlock. Police shot and killed the attacker, who had 35 rounds remaining in his gun.

RESTAURANTS

- On the morning of April 28, 1996, Martin Bryant, killed an elderly couple at the Seascape guesthouse, which his father had tried unsuccessfully to buy. Around 1:30 he went to the Broad Arrow Cafe at the Port Arthur Prison Colony Historic Site, a popular tourist attraction in Tasmania, Australia, for lunch. He ate his lunch on the deck and then reentered the cafe. Blocking the door so people couldn't leave, Bryant pulled an AR-15 and a FN-FAL .308 from his bag and began firing. He shot and killed 12 at the cafe and then moved to the adjacent gift shop, where he killed another 10 people. The shooting in the cafe and gift shop areas took about a minute.

  Bryant then left the building and headed for his car. En route, he killed several more people, including a mother and her two small children at point-blank range. At the tollbooth, he carjacked a BMW, killing the four passengers, and headed back to the guesthouse where the spree had begun. Along the way he saw a man and a woman in a Toyota stopped at a gas station. He stopped, forced the man into the trunk of the BMW, killed the woman, and drove back to the guesthouse, where he barricaded himself and his hostage inside. It was about 2:00.

  Two police officers arrived about two hours later, but Bryant pinned them in a ditch area with gunfire. A Tasmanian special police unit arrived about six hours later, but an 18-hour standoff ensued because the police didn't know that the hostage and the couple who owned the guesthouse were already dead. When

Spree Killings in Public Places

Bryant set the guesthouse on fire and ran outside, police captured him. All total, Bryant murdered 35 people that day.

The Port Arthur massacre remains Australia's single deadliest shooting spree. Australia had experienced 13 mass shootings in the previous 15 years. Twelve days after Bryant's killings, Australia enacted strict gun-control laws. At the time of the killings, Bryant was on disability because of being mentally handicapped.

- On October 16, 1991, George Hennard used a truck and a Glock 17 auto pistol to kill 22 and wound 20 at Luby's Cafeteria in Killeen, Texas. Hennard drove his truck through the front window of the cafeteria and then jumped out of the truck and began shooting. Some diners initially went to help the driver after the crash, only to be shot at. People were shot as they ran, hid behind tables, and crouched on the floor. The shooting, which lasted 12 minutes, ended when a police officer shot Hennard as he was attempting to shoot another victim. Hennard then fatally shot himself.

  Reportedly, Hennard yelled that his actions were "payback" as he shot people. He hadn't been diagnosed with or treated for mental illness, but those who knew him said that he had an intense dislike for women (his victims, however, were both male and female). Accounts also speculated that the killer was influenced by a documentary that he had seen on James Huberty, the gunman who killed 22 people and injured 19 at a MacDonald's in San Ysidro, California, in 1984. Hennard also had a ticket stub in his pocket for the movie *Fisher King,* which featured a shooting rampage at a restaurant. This is an instance where the media may have influenced the killer's actions.

  The Luby massacre prompted the Texas legislature to pass a law making it easier for citizens to get concealed carry permits.

WORKPLACE VIOLENCE

The workplace is the scene of almost 1 million violent crimes each year. About 10 percent of these violent crimes involve offenders armed with handguns. No job site, blue collar or white collar, is immune. After every downturn in the economy that necessitates layoffs, we see a spike in workplace killings.

In the workplace, experts have suggested three triggers that could initiate a violent response, the three Ds of workplace violence: discipline, demotion, and discharge. I have added a fourth: disrespect. (Incidentally, the next chapter shows how these same triggers apply to students.) I continue to be amazed by the way business management treats customers and employees. With all we know today about the importance of treating people in a respectful manner, we continue to see very poor interpersonal relations. A negative verbal approach often can easily ignite a physical confrontation, especially when dealing with an emotionally fragile person. The following are just a few of the notable examples of workplace violence.

- On April 17, 2009, Mario Ramirez, 50, a pharmacy technician at the Long Beach Memorial Medical Center in Southern California, shot and killed two supervisors at the hospital before killing himself with a handgun. No motive was established for the killings. Ramirez had worked at the hospital for 20 years and was well liked by coworkers.

- On July 2, 2004, Elijah Brown, 21, shot seven coworkers, killing five, at a Kansas City, Kansas, meatpacking plant and then killed himself. Three of the victims were from the same family, and it is believed that Brown had had an argument with one of them. It isn't known what set him off that day, but several people at the ConAgra plant described the gunman as strange, and said that he was bothered by teasing from coworkers. He seemed selective about his victims. He had no previous criminal record.

- On August 27, 2003, Salvador Tapia, 36, went to the Chicago warehouse company from which he had been fired six months before, and killed six former coworkers with a semiautomatic handgun. He died in a shootout with police. Tapia, who had a criminal record, was said to be angry about his termination.

- On July 8, 2003, Doug Williams, 48, shot 14 coworkers, killing six, with a 12-gauge shotgun at a Lockheed Martin assembly plant in Meridian, Mississippi. Williams was known to hold racist views, and eight of his shooting victims were black. Williams had left the plant during a meeting and returned armed with a shotgun, a rifle, and bandoleers of ammunition. The spree lasted about 10 minutes. He appeared to target victims based on their race and those he believed had complained about his racist threats to management.

- On February 5, 2001, William Baker, 66, a former employee who had worked at the Navistar International engine plant in Melrose Park, Illinois, before being fired for stealing, shot and killed four people. He then shot himself, but he survived the suicide attempt. Baker had previously pleaded guilty to theft and was scheduled to report to jail the next day to begin serving his five-month sentence. He had worked at the plant for 39 years. Baker is black, again unusual for a spree killer.

- On December 26, 2000, software engineer Michael McDermott, 42, killed seven coworkers at Edgewater Technology in Wakefield, Massachusetts. McDermott was armed with an AK-47 variant, a 12-gauge shotgun, and a .32-caliber pistol. After his killing spree, McDermott waited calmly for police to arrest him. Prosecutors claimed that McDermott was angry about the company's compliance with an order from the Internal Revenue Service to withhold part of his salary for back taxes. McDermott claimed that he was mentally ill and that he believed he had been "sent back in time to kill Nazis." He was convicted of seven counts of first-degree murder and sentenced to life in prison without possibility of parole.

Surviving a Massacre, Rampage, or Spree Killing

- On July 29, 1999, Mark Barton, 44, went on a rampage at two Atlanta day-trading brokerage firms after his trading rights were revoked, killing nine and injuring 12. Barton first went to his office and started shooting, and then crossed the street to another office and continued his rampage. He left the scene and later committed suicide when confronted by police. Hours after this rampage, his wife and two children were found dead in their home, where Barton had killed them before going to the trading firms to continue his killing spree. In total, Barton killed 12 people.

  Though never charged, police in Cherokee County, Alabama, considered Barton a suspect in the 1993 murders of his first wife and her mother. In his suicide note in the 1999 murders, Barton denied the 1993 murders.

Experts say the best way to prevent workplace violence is *not* to hire problem people in the first place. A thorough interview process and reference check could prevent the hiring of some potentially violent workers, but it won't solve the problem of workplace violence. Management and employees need to be vigilant about any warning signs of violence and share those concerns right away with authorities.

GOVERNMENT, POLITICAL, AND JUDICIAL BUILDINGS

Federal and state government workers, who make up 8 percent of the total U.S. workforce, account for 30 percent of all workplace victims. One government workplace in particular, the U.S. Postal Service, has developed a reputation for rampage shootings, and the term "going postal" has become a common term for going on a rampage. (However, when you consider the numbers of people employed by the post office system, it doesn't seem to have any more incidents than comparable job sites.) Since 1986, 10 people have killed postal workers or customers in Texas, Florida, California, Wisconsin, Michigan, New Jersey, and Oklahoma. Below are the two deadliest postal rampages.

Spree Killings in Public Places

- On January 30, 2006, Jennifer Sanmarco, 44, one of the few female mass shooters (according to research, from 1976 to 2004 the vast majority—more than 90 percent—of spree killers who used guns were male), killed six at the Goleta, California, mail-processing plant, where she had worked three years earlier. Sanmarco had a history of psychological problems, including making racist statements, and had been removed from the postal facility in 2003 because she was "acting strangely." She was put on disability because supervisors thought she would be a danger to herself. Sanmarco, who was white, is believed to have targeted her victims based on race: three African Americans, one Chinese American, one Filipino, and one Caucasian. She gained entry to the heavily secured facility by driving in behind an employee and stealing a badge. After the shootings, she killed herself. Before she went to the postal facility, Sanmarco had killed a former neighbor with whom she had argued back when they lived in the same complex.

  Despite a long history of mental illness, Sanmarco was able to purchase the gun she used in the shootings in New Mexico, where she had been living.

- The deadliest postal incident occurred on August 20, 1986, in Edmond, Oklahoma, when part-time letter carrier Patrick Sherrill, 44, killed 14 and injured six before committing suicide. Sherrill's strange behavior on and off the job had affected his relationships with his coworkers. In fact, he had been reprimanded the afternoon before the rampage, and one of the people he killed was one of the two supervisors who had spoken with him (the other was not at the location when the shooting began). As he walked through the workplace, Sherrill locked doors behind him so that postal employees couldn't escape. Some of the wounded survived by playing dead. The rampage lasted about 15 minutes before Sherrill ended it by committing suicide. There had been numerous complaints of Sherrill's unstable behavior and his hostility toward his coworkers.

Surviving a Massacre, Rampage, or Spree Killing

Of course, postal facilities aren't the only government buildings where violence occurs. The incidents described below involve murders at a state political headquarters, a city hall, and a county courthouse.

- On August 15, 2008, Timothy Dale Johnson, 50, fatally shot and killed Bill Gwatney, the chairman of the Arkansas Democratic Party, at the party headquarters in Little Rock. Police later killed Johnson after a 30-mile chase. Johnson had just quit (or was fired from) his job at a Target store. At his home, police found a Post-It note with Gwatney's last name and phone number, plus 14 guns. Johnson didn't shoot any one else at the party headquarters and asked for Gwatney by name. No motive is known.

- On February 9, 2008, Charles Thornton, 52, went on a deadly shooting spree at a city council meeting in Kirkwood, Missouri. He killed six people, including two police officers, two city council members, a city worker, and a news reporter. He also shot the mayor twice in the head, critically injuring him. Thornton was killed in a shootout with police, and a suicide note was found on his bed.

  Thornton was no stranger to city council meetings; he was twice convicted of disorderly conduct for disrupting the meetings. Thornton had a long-standing feud with the city, having received 150 tickets against his business, which he believed was being targeted unfairly because he was black. In reality, his trucks were ticketed because he parked them overnight in residential areas where commercial parking was illegal. Thornton had also just lost a federal free-speech lawsuit against the St. Louis suburb.

You might ask, what could be safer than a courthouse? Courthouses have metal detectors, police officers, and security—how could a murder happen there? The truth is that an assortment of bad people go into the courthouse every day, and some are very emotionally disturbed. In addition, friends and family of victims are also often in an emotional state. The courthouse offers friends of criminals a better opportunity to help someone escape than a jail does. While it might be difficult to bring a gun into a courthouse, it is possible to jump one of the officers in court who is armed and take his (or her, in this case) weapon, as we see in the following example.

- On March 11, 2005, 33-year-old Brian Nichols, on trial for rape and aggravated assault, murdered a judge, a court reporter, a sheriff's deputy, and a federal agent in a successful attempt to escape the Fulton County Courthouse in Atlanta, Georgia. The circumstances of this attack are a little different than the usual spree killing. Nichols had an extensive criminal record, and he was black. Plus, he wasn't suicidal. But like most spree killings, this one was planned.

  Nichols' friends warned authorities that he planned to escape, and Judge Barnes ordered extra security in his courtroom for the day Nichols was scheduled to testify. But he never testified. Instead, he overpowered the female deputy who was escorting from the bus to a holding cell in the courthouse. When she unlocked one of his handcuffs so that he could change into civilian clothes, he attacked her and took her gun and radio and then went in search of Judge Barnes. He found the judge and killed him, the court reporter, and a deputy before fleeing the courthouse. He later killed a federal agent while trying to steal his car. He was apprehended 26 hours later, when he surrendered at the apartment of a woman he had taken hostage. She was unharmed.

RELIGIOUS INSTITUTIONS

A church might be the last place you'd think of for a killing spree. You would be wrong. Churches attract a variety of people for an assortment of reasons. Some come because they have problems and are looking for answers. Clergy members often act as mediators to families in crisis, and sometimes one party takes exception to the advice. This can cause trouble. Many churches are getting concerned about this violence and have begun to implement safety precautions. I am currently working with one of the largest churches on Long Island, New York, to train more than 100 ushers and security personnel on how to recognize potentially dangerous people and defuse violent situations.

Below are a few examples of church shootings in the United States during the past 10 years.

- On March 8, 2009, Terry J. Sedlacek, 27, entered the First Baptist Church in Maryville, Illinois, and shot and killed its pastor, Rev. Fred Winters, while he was conducting a sermon. Winters' bible deflected the first shot, but the next three found their mark. At first, the worshippers thought this was part of the program, so they didn't react right away. But they soon realized that this was real. As Sedlacek walked down the center aisle, his handgun jammed, so he pulled out a knife. As two congregants struggled to restrain him, Sedlacek stabbed them and himself multiple times.

  Sedlacek only killed one person, but the body count probably would have been higher if his gun hadn't jammed—he had three magazines of 10 rounds each for the gun. The attack was planned, according to police, as indicated by a note found in a planner in his home that described that Sunday as "Death Day." After the attack, Sedlacek was diagnosed with schizophrenia and deemed unfit to stand trial. He had exhibited signs of mental instability before the attacks, which his family attributed to a bout of Lyme's disease.

- On May 17, 2008, Fernando Diaz Jr., 45, armed with a .22-caliber rifle, shot three people, including his ex-girlfriend, at a carnival outside St. John Baptist de la Salle, a Roman Catholic Church in Granada Hills, California. Diaz was angry about a custody dispute involving his 9-year-old son. The child was at the carnival with his mother, Diaz's primary target. Diaz carried a duffle bag in which he had hidden the rifle. Bystanders were able to tackle him when he stopped to reload, or because of a malfunction of his rifle (accounts differ), and hold him until police arrived. There were no fatalities.

- On December 8, 2007, Matthew Murray, 24, shot and killed two people at a Youth with a Mission training center outside Denver, Colorado, and then 12 hours later killed two more at New Life Church in Colorado Springs (70 miles south), which is affiliated with the Youth with a Mission program. At the Colorado Springs church, Murray detonated a smoke grenade to distract security people, causing a panic riot among the parishioners. After being shot five times by a female security guard, who was an off-duty police officer, Murray killed himself. According to police reports, Murray had been a student at the school before being dismissed in 2002 for unspecified "health reasons." Murray came from a deeply religious family and was home-schooled. He had no criminal record and no indication that he had been treated for mental illness. He had a rifle and two handguns on him when he died.

- On March 13, 2005, Terry Ratzmann, 44, walked into a suburban Milwaukee, Wisconsin, Sheraton Hotel, where an evangelical group associated with The Living Church of God was meeting. Ratzmann shot anyone in his way, leaving seven dead and four wounded, including the pastor and his son. Ratzmann then killed himself. The shooter was about to lose his job, and he was upset about a sermon the minister had delivered two weeks before. Ratzmann had struggled with depression for years.

- On September 15, 1999, Larry Gene Ashbroke, 47, entered the Wedgewood Baptist Church in Fort Worth, Texas, where 150 teens were gathered for a prayer service. He opened fire with a 9mm semiautomatic and a .380-caliber handgun, killing seven and injuring seven before killing himself.

Surviving a Massacre, Rampage, or Spree Killing

Ashbroke threw a pipe bomb at the front of the church before the attack, but it did little damage, and police found the materials for making more bombs in his home. The killer left no suicide note or writings to explain his actions. According to police, Ashbroke was "a very emotionally disturbed person"; his family described him as a paranoid schizophrenic. He was chronically unemployed. He had no connection with the church, and no one knows why he targeted its congregation.

MILITARY ESTABLISHMENTS

One of the last places you might expect a rampage shooting is on a military base. Security is tight, occupants are very disciplined and most have had background checks, and the ability to carry guns is limited. In spite of all that, on November 6, 2009, Maj. Nidal Hasan, 39, a U.S. Army psychiatrist who was treating veterans returning from Afghanistan and Iraq, opened fire at Fort Hood, Texas. Hasan killed 13 and wounded another 31. The attack occurred at the Soldier Readiness Center, where troops deploying to Iraq and Afghanistan receive last-minute medical checkups.

The soldiers inside were primarily unarmed and tried to stop him by throwing chairs at him and charging him, but against a heavily armed shooter, they were outmatched. Luckily, a trained female civilian police officer, in spite of being shot several times, was able to take Hasan down. It is believed that Hasan, a Muslim, was influenced by his religious feelings to execute the worst terror attack on U.S. soil since 9-11 and the worst shooting ever at a U.S. military base. In the past, Hasan had spoken out against the wars in both Afghanistan and Iraq and sought unsuccessfully to get a discharge from the military. It appears that the military hierarchy ignored a number of red flags. Was this because of political correctness? If so, this situation needs to be fixed.

CHAPTER 3

SPREE KILLINGS IN SCHOOLS

This chapter is intended to make educators, parents, and students aware of the dangers that both students and staff face these days. At times, you may find my criticism a bit harsh about how schools have dealt with safety issues in the past, but I feel it is well deserved. The role of educators is to create a safe environment for students to learn. The concept of *in loco parentis* (in the place of a parent) passes the responsibility for student safety to educators while the children are attending school or any school-sponsored function. In my opinion, one of the greatest deterrents to improved academic performance is an unsafe school.

I know that many of you sincerely believe that your local school is safe. That is exactly the answer you would have gotten from parents, students, and staff alike at Columbine High School only days before that massacre. The same would have been said about the Amish school in Lancaster County, Pennsylvania; Westside Middle School in Jonesboro, Arkansas; or Virginia Tech in Blacksburg, Virginia, beforehand. So keep an open mind as you read this chapter.

What concerns me most is that information about shootings, riots, or other safety issues never gets proper attention from the public. "College- and high school–based shooting incidents continue across the country, though they aren't making the evening news. With the exception of regional news, many of the shootings didn't make the headlines" (*Law and Order*, June 2009). When the public and educators are unaware of the extent of these events, there is no motivation to do something about the problem.

For this book, I have elected to treat K-12 schools (primarily high schools, but there have also been murders at middle schools, and the one-room Amish school in Pennsylvania had K-12 students) and colleges separately because of the differences in campus layout and distribution of the buildings, as well as the age difference. I believe it is important to see the entire scope of school violence, so I have included several examples of international school killings. Acts of international violence are no longer isolated incidents. Today, what happens anywhere in the world could influence the next attack here, and vice versa. Who would have thought that the Columbine duo would be heroes and role models for future school shooters nationally and internationally? Studying these events in other parts of the world will help us better understand the who, the why, and the how of school shootings, as well as to realistically gauge how some of these global events might influence killers in our schools in the future.

SCHOOL KILLINGS

According to a joint study by the U.S. Department of Education's National Center for Education Statistics, its Institute of Education Sciences, and the Bureau of Justice Statistics, students between the ages of 12 and 18 were victims of 1.7 million violent and nonviolent crimes at schools during the 2006–2007 school year (*Education Week*, April 29, 2009). Unfortunately, this study didn't seem to separate the violent from nonviolent crime, and this is very important to know. Eight percent of the students in grades 9 through 12 reported having been threatened or injured with a weapon in the previous 12 months.

These figures are bad enough by themselves, but I don't believe they represent the real extent of school violence. This data comes from what is reported by school districts. Having worked closely with teachers from hundreds of districts, I have heard too many stories about administrators or school boards suppressing information on violence. Plus, school reports often don't include any acts of violence by students outside the buildings.

According to a student survey of 2,000-plus students conducted by Alfred University's division of school psychology, about 10 percent of the nation's 7th through 12th graders may have tendencies to behave violently, and 2.6 percent could be considered dangerous because they have both an inclination toward violence and the means to commit it. In a high school of about 800, that's 20 students likely to actually carry out violent actions.

The students seem to know who in their school is capable of violence and what might drive them to it, with 87 percent citing revenge as the strongest motivation. Roughly 75 percent of the students said they were concerned about a shooting happening at their school—and according to the survey, they have good reason to be concerned. Most disturbing is the fact that only 50 percent said they would tell an adult if they overheard a student talking about shooting someone. We have to do something about awakening students' obligation to make school safer for themselves and their peers. Silence Hurts is a national campaign by Media Partners that tries to get students to break the code of silence and tell authorities if something wrong is happening in the school.

For more information about school shooters, check out Peter Langman's *Why Kids Kill: Inside the Minds of School Shooters.* Langman is the clinical director of a group called KidsPeace, a charity-based group that provides mental health services for children and teens in 11 states. This is exactly the approach I recommend that communities take to help young people with problems.

Overt vs. Covert

School violence generally falls into two categories, overt and covert. Overt violence includes fights, riots, shootings, bombings, and so forth. Covert violence, on the other hand, includes bullying, racism, homophobia, disrespect, extortion, and threats. Covert violence can be difficult to recognize, especially if the staff isn't properly trained. It is also easy to ignore. While less frequent, overt violence gets our attention more quickly and is acted on immediately as opposed to covert violence. What many educators fail to realize is that the far more common covert violence eventually triggers overt violence. In my opinion, the only reason bullying became such a big issue in schools was because of the overt violence it occasionally elicited. The suffering of the "victims" of covert violence seemed secondary.

Hazing can be a form of overt or covert violence. It is less of a problem at the K-12 level than at colleges. Still, being hazed to join a group does occur in some high schools, and it often goes unnoticed or ignored by educators. Some hazing is relatively harmless, but some young people have been seriously hurt or killed in the process. Hazing rituals might include drinking, fighting, or other criminal activity.

My experience has shown me that every school has its share of covert violence, and very little is being done to deal with it realistically. Schools are forced to act when violence is overt, and even then the actions are more to make parents, students, and the community feel like steps have been taken to ensure that it can't happen again. I want to share something that was told to me in the early 1990s by Dr. Arun Gandhi, the director of the Gandhi Institute on Nonviolence: "If we want to prevent overt violence, we must first deal with covert violence." I agree completely.

Why So Much Teen Violence?

I am amazed when I hear adults, educators, and criminal justice workers ponder why there is so much violence among our youth. Having worked with teenagers, I sometimes am amazed that they survive at all. Teens experience the extremes of joy and unhappiness, with joy often switching to unhappiness in the blink of an eye.

Children are born with certain instinctive drives to ensure survival, such as grabbing food and protecting what they believe is their property. But in terms of other behaviors, they come with a blank slate (*tabula rosa*). They must learn to be honest and to share. They must learn not to hit, fight, or cheat. They learn these values from their family members, their educators, their cultural and religious institutions, and their peers. In some cultures, children are being raised to be suicide bombers; they are taught that killing others who hold different religious or cultural views is righteous.

Unfortunately, our institutional safety systems are loaded with cracks, through which many students fall. It is only when kids act out violently that they get our full attention. We are seeing more kids who are fatherless or motherless, fearless, godless, and remorseless.

Reasons for the Increase in Violence

Children are exposed to a number of positive and negative factors that affect their development. When the positive forces are working, there is some balance. When some fail, other factors, mostly negative, become dominant. The five primary influences on children are family, community (religious institutions), school, peers, and the media. I discussed some of these influences earlier, but here I'd like to delve a little more into how specifically they affect children.

Family Influence

Most often, the primary influence in a child's life is the family. Unfortunately, in the United States, we are seeing deterioration in the family unit, which causes catastrophic problems for young people. More and more children are being brought up in broken families and dysfunctional homes, where physical, sexual, or emotional abuse is common. When the family unit begins to fail, for whatever reason, it places greater emphasis on the remaining four factors. Because of the importance of the family, I feel strongly that schools should provide parenting classes to parents and students. For parents, we need to provide guidance and programs to help them cope with their children (especially teens). Plus, we want teens to recognize the reality of raising a family *before* they start having children of their own. Maybe this will help the next generation of children.

According to Gene Watson, retired police chief, Grand Island, Nebraska, "We keep creating criminals and wonder why there's crime and violence" (*Law and Order*, September 1999). Children who watch their mothers being abused often develop deep emotional problems that manifest in violence, often in bullying behavior that escalates into abuse. Many abusers are bullies who were never helped. On the other hand, these bullies are often a factor in school shooting sprees, either as the specific target or the impetus for random killing. Studies have shown that bullies are more likely to become delinquents and adult criminals. Saddest of all, we have known for quite some time that abused and neglected children are more likely to be arrested for juvenile delinquency, adult crimes, and violent behavior. These are the delinquents that many people are demanding we lock up.

Community Influence

The next factor is the influence of the community in which the child lives, which includes religious institutions. Unfortunately, when the family falls apart, we generally see the positive community influence go as well, unless a concerned adult picks up the slack. Too often, this doesn't happen.

School Influence

Another important influence in a child's life is the school. Again, if the family fails, the school often loses influence also. Once again, that is, unless a concerned adult, such as a teacher, coach, or guidance counselor, picks up the slack.

Peer Influence

Peers and the pressure they exert have a tremendous impact on young people. Too often, peer pressure takes up the slack when the first three factors fail. This has given rise to the growth of street gangs, which become the family unit. Unfortunately, more often than not, this influence is negative. It could include (but isn't limited to) use of drugs and alcohol, unprotected sex, teenage parenthood, and criminal behavior, including murder.

Spree Killings in Schools

Media Influence

Many experts are beginning to acknowledge the power of the media on everyone, but especially on young people. The media greatly influences the role models teens choose to look and act like, but it is often irresponsible in what they promote to young people. Kids are exposed to R- and X-rated movies, music, websites, and games before they can comprehend the consequences of certain behaviors.

One of the media influences I feel very strongly about is how violent video games affect developing children. Many of the video games targeted at teenagers represent the dark side of human nature, promoting death, rape, violence, and mayhem. These games desensitize young people to the value of human life by teaching them how to shoot to kill and other combat skills. They learn some of the same techniques taught to military and law enforcement professionals. Lacking the maturity and discipline that adults have, some of these youngsters are walking time bombs. It is my belief that we have only begun to see the extent of this problem in schools.

The producers of such violent video games as *Postal* and *Super Columbine Massacre* argue that it is their First Amendment right to make their games available and that their inclusion of a rating system, which clearly states that this content is intended for adults, absolves them of the responsibility of underage children playing these games. They say, with some justification, that it is the parents' responsibility to monitor what games their children are playing. Some parents are either naive or stupid enough to buy these games for their kids. Once one kid has a game, his friends are not far behind.

The following is a shocking example of two powerful forces at work in a negative way: peer influence and the media. Inspired by the *Grand Theft* video, six teens in Nassau County, New York, went on an all-night crime spree with a bat, a crowbar, and stick. They robbed and beat up a man, knocking him to the ground, and then kicked him repeatedly and knocked out several of his teeth. They then tried to carjack a vehicle and smashed a van with a bat. The teens told detectives they were imitating the video game. (*Newsday* June 27, 2008.)

Surviving a Massacre, Rampage, or Spree Killing

Mental Illness

This might be the most important influence of all in the behavior of school spree killers. Several studies by prominent groups have suggested that a significant number of students suffer from some form of mental illness, which largely goes untreated.

Antisocial or violent behavior is actually first seen in elementary school. According to FBI behavioral sciences experts, teachers in elementary school are usually the first to see sociopathic behavior. The question is what do they do with this information? Most schools fail to address this issue because of expense, lack of training, and not seeing it as their job. Teachers (often with instruction from the administration) simply push people (and problems) along to the next grade, and they become someone else's problem. I have heard this firsthand. By the time these troubled young people reach junior high school and the hormones kick in, they become increasingly dangerous to themselves and others. The middle school is where the greatest number of assaults on students and teachers occurs.

A 16-year-old minor in Novo Hamburgo, Brazil, acknowledged to police in what was described as a "chillingly calm confession" that he had killed 12 people over the course of three months. He said he killed in "fits of rage" or out of revenge. In one case, he killed because the victim wanted to date his sister. He would shoot a victim in the head and riddle their bodies with bullets. The boy is an unemployed high school dropout. (*Newsday,* March 29, 2008.) Did the school have any indication of his problems at an earlier age, when he might have been helped? What about his parents? By the time he was 16, someone must (or should) have noticed that something was seriously wrong with him.

According to Dr. Dewey G. Cornell of the University of Virginia, violent juveniles fall into three categories, and they are all dangerous. One group consists of the psychotic and delusional. The second group has a long history of disruptive or delinquent behavior. With attentive parents or attentive educators, young people in these two groups should be identified and, hopefully, helped before they do something

Spree Killings in Schools

really terrible. Unfortunately, either because of apathy, denial, or a lack of training, too often these young people are allowed to spiral down and eventually explode violently. People in the third group give no warning. They never say or do anything that warrants attention until they go on a rampage. This makes it especially difficult to predict violent behavior in this group. (*Law and Order,* June 2009.)

We have seen the strong link between suicide and homicide, and how this relates to spree killers. A study by Columbia University's Carmel Hill Center for the Early Diagnosis and Treatment of Mental Illness suggests school-based health centers should offer voluntary mental health screenings to all teens, and parents should work with schools to ensure that their kids have at least one checkup before graduating from high school. The report's statistics about teen depression are staggering: more than 800,000 teenagers each year are diagnosed as suffering from depression, and more than 500,000 teenagers attempt an act of suicide that requires medical intervention. The report states that suicide is the third leading cause of death among 15- to 19-year-olds.

Poor Judgment

Kids get into trouble because they typically show poor judgment, even "good" kids. Pressure to do something stupid is all around them. Shows on cable TV like *Jackass* and *Scarred* are quite popular among young people. If you think watching kids break bones and get concussions might discourage young people from trying these extreme activities, you are wrong. Sometimes a student's reckless behavior results in injury to the student, but it can also be directed at others.

Why do most 16-year-olds drive like they're missing a part of their brain? An All-State ad in *U.S. News and World Report* reveals that even bright, mature teens sometimes do stupid things because their brains *haven't* fully developed, and may not until they reach their mid-20s. The underdeveloped area, the dorsal lateral prefrontal cortex, plays a crucial role in decision making, problem solving, and understanding the consequences of their behavior. So expecting a teenager to think like an adult and make the same mature decisions is unrealistic on the part of parents and educators.

Hormones

Hormones play an important part in the drives of teenagers. A lot has been written about the effects of testosterone, but much less is written about the effects of estrogen. Humans are the only animals expected to delay mating five to ten years after puberty sets in. How realistic is this? Abstinence takes tremendous discipline, something not commonly found in teens. Hormones are extremely powerful and often cloud judgment. In males, hormones make them very competitive with other males. Combine this competitiveness with lethal weapons, and the results are often tragic—and final.

Substance Abuse

The problem of substance abuse among teenagers is out of control. Alcohol is still one of the most commonly abused substances, probably because of easy availability. I'm not talking about having a drink or two, but rather "binge" drinking. This often starts even before high school, and it is very common in college. Some studies suggest that 50 percent of college males and 30 percent of college females binge drink. Additionally, marihuana and other stronger illegal substances are being used on high school campuses. At "pharming" parties, the latest attempt at getting high, young people randomly mix prescription drugs, often with lethal effects.

If you add weapons into this mix of poor judgment, hormones, substance abuse, and peer pressure, you have a recipe for disaster.

What Can Be Done to Prevent Future Violence?

Supervision Is Key

As teens get older, they are given greater amounts of freedom. This is part of the natural separation process from their parents to get them ready for college or life on their own. During this time, they frequently spend more unsupervised time at home and go out with their friends to destinations unknown to their parents. Too much freedom, too soon, can spell trouble for any child. Bad things happen (or are planned) between the hours of 3 and 6 in the afternoon, when supervision is almost nonexistent for many teens with working parents.

Most parents think that "poor parenting" means being abusive or negligent. Being too permissive is also detrimental to children. Parents assume their kids can make decisions that are in their long-term best interest, and they can't, as we saw earlier. You are *not* your children's friend; you're their parent, and as such you must make the decisions that are in their best interests, even if they disagree. They won't like you for it, but you must monitor their Internet activity, video games, and TV programs. Make sure you know where they spend their time and with whom. Get to know their friends, *and their parents*.

Educators must be much better trained in antiviolence efforts. They need to be able to recognize covert violence and how it leads to overt violence. They must recognize the importance of adult supervision *everywhere* on the school campus. At no time should students be left unsupervised. It is during the unsupervised periods that the bullies, extortionists, and troublemakers take over. Unfortunately, I have had this discussion with administrators and teachers on numerous occasions, and I have gotten lots of excuses about why it is impossible to do this *all* the time.

Learn from Past Examples

Studying past school shootings could be helpful in preventing them in the future. The following are some of the horrific examples of school rampages in the United States and elsewhere.

- Columbine High School in Littleton, Colorado, wasn't the first school shooting in the United States, but it was the first to play out on live television. The whole nation watched stunned on April 20, 1999, as senior students Eric Harris, 18, and Dylan Klebold, 17, carried out their massacre, which left 12 students and one teacher dead and 23 students injured. Even now, more than 10 years later, Columbine is still the most infamous (and most imitated) school rampage in the world.

There were many red flags before the killings at Columbine for those who were trained to see them. For those who weren't so trained, Klebold and Harris appeared to be normal teens. They worked together in a pizza parlor, liked to play the computer game *Doom* in the afternoons, and worried about finding a date for the prom. However, they found it difficult to fit into any of the groups at the high school. Athletes and other students frequently picked on them. From notes and videos that Klebold and Harris left behind, authorities learned that Klebold had been thinking of suicide as early as 1997, and they both began thinking about a large massacre as early as April 1998. On the front of his journal, Harris wrote, "I hate the fucking world." This was a full year before the killings.

As part of their plea agreement after a van break-in in April 1998, the two were forced to enroll in a juvenile diversion program, where they attended workshops, spoke with counselors, worked on volunteer projects, and convinced everyone they were sorry. Meanwhile, during the entire time they were in the program, they were planning a large-scale massacre at their high school. So, the two fooled even the "experts" working with them. After the shootings, experts labeled Harris as a psychopath with multiple-personality problems. When information about the shooters was made public in 2006, it revealed that Klebold showed signs of psychosis and displayed symptoms of depression, hopelessness, and rage.

Klebold and Harris had a small group of friends known as the "Trench Coat Mafia," even though they didn't usually wear trench coats to school. On April 20, Harris and Klebold both wore their long coats—to hide the weapons they were carrying. Harris and Klebold planned to kill as many people as possible the day of the attack and then kill themselves. They had used the

Spree Killings in Schools

Internet to find recipes for pipe bombs and other explosives and amassed an arsenal that eventually included guns, knives, and 99 explosive devices. They had studied the movement of students and found that there would be more than 500 students in the cafeteria at 11:15, when the first lunch period began. They had planted a propane bomb in the cafeteria, which was timed to explode at 11:17 (it failed to detonate), and then they planned to shoot survivors as they ran out. Additionally, they had pipe bombs but didn't use them.

When the shooting first started, students thought it was a prank. When reality set in, panic erupted. Ten students were killed in the cafeteria in the first 7 1/2 minutes. The terror spread to other parts of the school and lasted 46 minutes before the two shooters committed suicide. As shocking as the attack was, it easily could have been much worse: if the propane bombs had detonated as planned and the pipe bombs been used, hundreds more could have been killed or injured. So luck played an important part this day. The sad news was that Columbine wasn't the last killing spree of its kind. Many more followed.

I believe that some observations about Columbine are in order here. Before the shooting, if anyone had interviewed the staff at Columbine, they would have received a glowing report about the school. This is because most staff members either weren't trained to see covert violence or they simply ignored it. There were plenty of troubling signs that should have been picked up by teachers, students, parents, and law enforcement professionals. Did elementary or middle school teachers not detect something about the boys' behavior that warranted further attention? Since there is no agreement about who is responsible for emotionally disturbed students, no one is. It had better become someone's responsibility.

- Seth Trickey, a 13-year-old student at Fort Gibson Middle School, in Fort Gibson, Oklahoma, was greatly influenced by the

Columbine shooters when he decided to take his father's 9mm semiautomatic handgun to school on December 6, 1999, to shoot his classmates. Outside the school, Trickey fired his gun at least 15 times, wounding five, before being subdued by a teacher. Fortunately, no one died in this incident, which occurred just eight months after Columbine

Trickey didn't match the profile of the Columbine shooters because he had been taking the prescription drug Inderal for migraines and had been referred to a psychologist for stress management training. A week before the shooting, Seth was suffering from poison ivy and received a large injection of the prescription drug Kenalog, a steroid alleged to have psychotic effects on some users. Some psychologists say that Seth's obsession with military tactics and his identification with Gen. George Patton might have caused him to see the attack as a way to test his field combat ability. Trickey was found guilty of shooting with intent to kill and having a weapon on school property. The judge recommended that the defendant receive clinical counseling at a facility for juvenile offenders, meaning he would be eligible to be back in school in less than two years.

- The massacre at the one-room West Nickel Mines Amish School in the Old Order Amish community of Nickel Mines in Lancaster County, Pennsylvania, shook the soul of the Amish community, and the nation, to its core. At approximately 10:25 A.M. on October 2, 2006, Charles Carl Roberts IV, a 32-year-old milk-truck driver who lived nearby, backed his truck up to the schoolhouse and entered. He asked the teacher and students if they had seen a lost clevis pin along the road. When they replied that they hadn't, he left and then returned armed with a 9mm semiautomatic.

The Amish massacre started as a hostage situation. Roberts forced the boys to help unload a variety of items from his truck, including a shotgun, a change of clothes, toilet paper, candles, sexual lubricant, and flexible plastic ties. While he was distracted with the unloading, the teacher and her mother, who was visiting the classroom that day, managed to escape and run to a nearby farm to call 911, at approximately 10:36. Roberts saw the women escaping and tried to stop them but failed. He then barricaded the front door and lined the children up against the chalkboard. He allowed a pregnant woman, three parents with infants, and all the boys to leave. Left behind were 10 female students (and a teacher's aide), whom he restrained with plastic ties.

The first police officer arrived at around 10:42. Other officers and medical personnel followed. Police opened communication with Roberts and told him to let the hostages go. He refused. When police heard the first shot at approximately 11:07, they stormed the building. But by the time they got inside, Roberts had killed five of the young girls and wounded five others (plus the teacher's aide) before committing suicide. Most of those killed were shot execution style in the back of the head. The victims ranged in age from 6 to 16.

Roberts' wife found suicide notes that he had left behind. There is no question that Roberts suffered from some form of mental illness, which some attributed to the death of his first child, a daughter who lived only 20 minutes.

Apparently, there was no way at the Amish school to communicate with the outside world quickly. It took approximately 10 minutes for the teacher to reach a farmhouse with a telephone and call 911, which allowed Roberts to fortify his position. Had the police been notified sooner, he might not have had time to barricade the doors, which might have allowed police to enter sooner and reduced the number of victims. One of the essentials I stress for schools is a good communication system in the event of an emergency of any kind. But the Amish people could never have foreseen a tragedy like this. Within days the Amish community called for forgiveness of the killer, and within the year it demolished the schoolhouse to get this violence out of their minds.

Roberts left four suicide notes, to his wife and three children.

Surviving a Massacre, Rampage, or Spree Killing

He was clearly emotionally disturbed. In one of the notes, he said that he was still angry with God over the death of his first-born child nine years earlier, the daughter who lived only 20 minutes.

- Many people may have never heard of—or may have forgotten—the massacre at Westside Middle School, a consolidated school outside Jonesboro, Arkansas, which happened a year *before* Columbine, on March 24, 1998. Westside was one of the first big school shootings in the United States. What was most shocking about the Westside shootings was the age of the shooters. Andrew Golden was 11 and Mitchell Johnson was 13 when they concocted their evil plan to kill fellow students and teachers at their middle school.

  The night before the shooting, the boys loaded Johnson's mother's van with survival gear, camping supplies, and 10 weapons, including two semiautomatic rifles, one bolt-action rifle, and seven handguns. Three handguns were from Golden's home and an additional four handguns and three rifles were stolen from Golden's grandfather. The next day the two, clad in camouflage clothing, arrived at Westside in the van. While Mitchell took the weapons to a field adjacent to the school, Golden pulled the fire alarm in the building, at 12:35, and then ran to join Mitchell. From where they waited, the two had a clear view of the exit doors the teachers and students would come out of for the fire drill. During the rampage, the two killed four female students and a teacher, and wounded nine other students and one teacher. Some speculated that the killers targeted specific students or teachers (in particular sixth-grade teacher Shannon Wright, who was killed), but that was never proven, and investigators concluded that any association between the shooters and victims was coincidental. The two boys tried to escape back to the van, which was parked about a half mile away, but were captured by the police. Golden and Johnson may have patterned their attack after an earlier one in Stamps, Arkansas, just three months earlier (December 15, 1997). Joseph "Colt" Todd, 14, hid in the woods by his high school and shot and wounded two students. Todd said that he shot the students because he was tired of being teased and bullied.

Golden and Johnson, who were in different grades, rode the same bus to and from school. Johnson's parents were divorced, and he lived with his mother and stepfather. He had a good relationship with his stepfather and siblings. Adults who knew him described him as quiet and respectful, and noted that he faithfully attended church and sang in the choir. On the other hand, students who knew him painted a much darker side. They described him as a braggart and a bully. They also said that he spoke of "having a lot of killing to do," and that he wanted to belong to a gang and smoke pot. But no student brought this to the attention of an adult before the shooting. Earlier that same year, he had been punished three times with in-school suspensions and had been charged with molesting a toddler (but this record was expunged because he was a minor). Both adults and students who knew Andrew Golden described a darker side. He apparently came from a stable family (ironically, both of his parents were postal workers). He once reportedly shot a classmate in the face with a pellet gun, and he was accused of killing a playmate's cat. (Many psychologists and criminal profilers have pointed out that serial killers often begin by killing animals.)

There were definite red flags that might have tipped off teachers, law enforcement, healthcare professionals, and parents, especially in the case of Golden. Also, the Golden family did a poor job of securing weapons they owned. We have to realize that with modern weapons, even small kids can be lethal.

While the boys professed their regret, other prisoners in the facility said they bragged about their crime. The two were among the youngest ever charged with murder in America. The prosecutor said if it weren't for their ages, he would have sought the death penalty. Instead they were sentenced to confinement until their 21st birthday. After his release in 2005, Johnson soon ran afoul of the law again on drug, firearms, and related charges, and is currently incarcerated. Golden changed his name and remained out of the public eye until he applied for a concealed carry permit in Arkansas in 2008. His request was refused.

The laws in Arkansas were changed after this case. If this occurred today, shooters of the same age would be charged as adults and sentenced to life in prison.

- On March 21, 2005, Jeff Weise, 17, an Ojibwa Indian, arrived on campus at Red Lake Senior High School, Minnesota, from which he had been expelled, and grinned and waved to students as he shot at them. Pleas by students for him to stop went unheeded. At the school he killed seven, including a teacher and a security guard, and wounded seven others. He exchanged fire with police briefly before killing himself. Before going to the school, Weise shot and killed his grandfather, Daryl Lussier Sr. and Lussier's girlfriend, Michelle Sigana, at their home on the Red Lake Indian Reservation. Weise's grandfather was a police officer with the Red Lake Police Department, which may be where Weise got his guns.

  Weise had a troubled background. His parents were never married, and he was shuttled between his father on the reservation and his mother, who lived in the Twin Cities area. When Jeff was 8, his father committed suicide; when he was 11, his mother suffered brain damage in a car accident and had to be put in a nursing home. At this time, Jeff came back to the reservation to live with his grandfather, where he remained until his death. He expressed frustration over having to live on the reservation, where he felt like an outsider.

  At school, he was frequently bullied but didn't respond. He wore black clothing and a black trench coat all year long and was considered a "Goth" by other students. In April 2004 when rumors swirled around Red Lake Senior High School that someone was planning a shooting rampage on the anniversary of

Spree Killings in Schools

Columbine, some faculty suspected him. In May 2004 he attempted suicide, and in the fall he was expelled from public school and placed in a home-schooling program. After his death, investigators found multiple postings on the Internet describing his troubled life and his dark thoughts.

KILLINGS ON COLLEGE CAMPUSES

Everyone knows about the shooting at Virginia Tech because it made the papers as the worst school mass killing on record. However, most people are unaware that this was not just an isolated incident and that it could happen again in their area. There is the real danger of this happening on many college campuses today. According to Michael Dorn, director of Safe Havens and a leading authority on school violence, "Colleges and universities, contrary to popular belief, have a higher incidence of weapons assaults than their K-12 counterparts" (*Police Magazine*, June 2007). This isn't the kind of information that colleges publicize, but it remains a fact. Here are just a few of the deadly rampages that have occurred on college campuses.

- On April 16, 2007, on the campus of Virginia Polytechnic Institute and State University (Virginia Tech) in Blacksburg, Virginia, Seung-Hui Cho, 23, killed 32 of his fellow students before committing suicide. According to the medical examiner, Cho fired more than 100 times, and victims were shot multiple times.

  Unlike many rampages, the assault at Virginia Tech lasted more than two hours and involved two separate locations: West Ambler Johnston Hall and Norris Hall. Just after 7:00 A.M., Cho killed two students at Johnston Hall (a residence hall, but not the one where Cho resided) and then left the scene. He returned to his dorm room, cleaned up, and prepared a package consisting of a video and an 1,800-word manifesto about the incident for NBC News. Cho left his dorm room and mailed the package at 9:01.

  Cho then walked to Norris Hall, which houses the engineering department, and resumed his rampage, about two hours after the initial shots. At Norris Hall, Cho peeked into a couple of classrooms before arriving at Room 206, where he killed the professor and nine students. He then went to Room 207, where he killed the professor and four more students. Hearing the gunshots, Professor Liviu Librescu and a couple of students barricaded the door to Room 204, which delayed Cho's entrance and saved lives. Librescu and one student physically held the door closed while the other students climbed out the window. Multiple shots through the door eventually killed Librescu (who had been a Holocaust survivor) and the student. Cho then moved on to Room 211, where the instructor and a student also held the door closed while students escaped through the window. Both the instructor and student in Room 211 also died of gunshot wounds. Cho then tried to enter Room 205, which had also been barricaded, but he could not get in. Cho reentered Rooms 206 and 207 and shot students who had survived the initial gunfire. About 10 or 12 minutes after entering Norris Hall, Cho shot and killed himself. At Norris Hall, he killed 25 students and five instructors in four different rooms.

Cho was a senior English major at Virginia Tech at the time of the shootings. Former classmates said Cho had experienced years of bullying as a teen because of his extreme shyness and the strange way he talked (he was of South Korean ancestry). While in high school, he had been diagnosed with severe anxiety disorder and received treatment. In college, Cho was described by classmates and professors as very quiet and troubled, and always alone. He had been accused of stalking two female students in the fall of 2005; after an investigation, he was declared mentally ill and ordered to seek treatment. Despite his record of mental illness, Cho was able to purchase the firearms he used in the rampage.

The massacre caused many people to question the lack of a campus-wide emergency alert system on college campuses, gun laws in the United States, the privacy laws that deny schools access to mental health records of their students, the treatment of mentally ill in general, and the way campus security and police officers handled this active shooter.

- On October 29, 2008, four men drove around the University of Central Arkansas (UCA) campus in Conway for several minutes before firing at least eight rounds from a semiautomatic pistol, killing two students and wounding a third. Police later said that the two killed were not the intended targets. The shooters, aged 19–20, all had criminal records. The gunmen were charged with two counts of murder and one count of attempted capital murder, plus eight lesser offenses. Police said that the shootings were not random.

  To illustrate how one event can trigger another, students at UCA were so jittery that when they saw campus police rushing across a courtyard the next day, they wondered whether to run for cover. A panic riot could have easily followed.

- On February 14, 2008, former student Steven Kazmierczak, 27, opened fire in a lecture hall at Northern Illinois University in DeKalb. There were between 150–200 students in the class when he began shooting. Kazmierczak was armed with three handguns, hidden under his coat, and a shotgun concealed in a guitar case. He killed five students and wounded 18 others before committing suicide.

  Kazmierczak was enrolled in graduate school at the University of Illinois, Urbana-Champaign, working on a degree in social work at the time of the shootings. He had a history of mental illness, beginning in high school, and was under psychiatric care at the time. His behavior was described as erratic in the weeks leading up to the killings, and it is believed that he had stopped taking his medications. He was described by faculty and students as an outstanding student, and he had a girlfriend. Some researchers reported that Kazmierczak had researched previous school shootings, including Columbine and Virginia Tech. He left no suicide note and removed the hard drive from his computer and a computer chip from his cell phone, so there is no record of his thoughts or motivation.

- On September 13, 2006, Kimveer Gil, 25, parked his car on a street near Dawson College, just outside Montreal, Quebec, and started unloading firearms. Gil took a passerby hostage and made him carry a bag containing the guns and ammunition onto the campus. When Gil began shooting on the steps of a rear entrance, the hostage escaped. Then Gil went into the cafeteria, set down his bag (which contained a pistol-caliber carbine, a 9mm handgun, and a short-barreled shotgun, all of which he legally owned), loaded a gun, and fired into the floor. He told the students to lie on the floor and began shooting them. Two police officers, who were on campus for an unrelated reason, heard the gunshots and rushed to the cafeteria. When he became aware of the police officers, he took two more hostages. After being shot in the arm by police, Gil killed himself. In the rampage, Gil fired 60 shots, killing one person and wounding 19. Police found a suicide note on his body.

  Those who knew Gil described him as a loner. He had posted several photos of himself on Internet sites, dressed in a black trench coat and holding guns and knives. He was said to have spent hours at a shooting range, practicing his marksmanship. He also kept an online journal, in which he recorded his dark thoughts, about his hatred of people and his love of guns. On one, he wrote that his preferred way to die was in a "hail of gunfire," and in another he described his mood as "homicidal."

FOILED PLOTS

Fortunately, many massacre plots are uncovered before they can be executed. In these cases, alert adults or students contacted the authorities once they suspected foul play.

Spree Killings in Schools

- Columbine provided the inspiration for Eric McKeehan, 17; his brother Michael, 15; and Steven Jones, 15, to plan a shooting and bombing attack on their high school in New Bedford, Massachusetts. The three boys wanted their massacre to be "bigger than Columbine." Fortunately, word got around school that some students were plotting to attack the school, and before they could carry out the attack, a school janitor discovered a letter discussing their plans to detonate explosions and then shoot students as they fled the building. The janitor turned over the letter to authorities, and law enforcement was brought into the picture. A search of the students' homes revealed bomb-making instructions, knives, shotgun shells, and photos of the suspects holding what appeared to be handguns. They planned to kill themselves as a "final solution" (sound familiar?). Authorities closed the school and brought in bomb-sniffing dogs to search the building.

  The next day when school reopened, attendance was poor. Threats like these, even bomb threats, usually results in poor attendance and a loss of valuable teaching time. The three students were charged with conspiracy to commit murder. The mother of one of the boys was quoted as saying, "It was just tough talk." That is a classic case of a parent in denial (*Newsday*, November 26, 2001).

- A 14-year-old boy plotted a Columbine bloodbath at his school in Lovejoy, Georgia. He drew up detailed plans to block fire exits, pull the alarm, and shoot people as they tried to leave. The plot began to unravel when students told authorities that the boy had tried to recruit others to participate. The police seized the boy's notebook, which had notes and diagrams of his planned attack, and charged him with making terrorist threats and conspiracy to commit murder. (*Newsday* October 2, 2003.)

- Police in Connecticut seized weapons from the home of Frank Fechteler, 16, a Newington High School student, after being tipped off by a parent of an alleged plot to attack the high school (*Newsday*, February 15, 2007). Fechteler was charged with manufacturing bombs. Documents seized in his home, as well as statements made by the teen, indicated that he had targeted specific students for death.

The parent who tipped off police saw a video on YouTube that claimed a teen was planning to attack the school in the next couple of months. While this parent acted responsibly, there was also an element of luck involved in his seeing the clip in time to prevent this attack. The big question is, when will our luck run out?

SAFE SCHOOL INITIATIVE REPORT

In its role as protector of the president of the United States and other elected officials and candidates, the Secret Service conducted an operational study called the Exceptional Case Study Project (ECSP), which reviewed all persons in the past 50 years who attacked or tried to attack a national leader or public figure. The investigators studied the behavior and thinking of these individuals with the goal of improving the approach to threat assessment—i.e., the process of identifying, assessing, and managing persons who may pose a risk to protectees before they approach or attack.

Because of their expertise in threat assessments, the Secretary of Education contacted officials of the Secret Service in 1999 following the Columbine massacre for guidance on preventing or reducing school killings. The staff of the Secret Service's newly formed National Threat Assessment Center agreed to conduct a similar operation of school shootings (or "targeted violence," in Secret Service language). For the project, dubbed the Safe School Initiative, NTAC studied 37 school shootings involving 41 attackers from 1974 through June 2000. The focus was on "examining the thinking, planning, and other behaviors engaged in by students who carried out school attacks. Particular attention was given to identifying pre-attack behaviors and communications that might be detectable—or

Spree Killings in Schools

'knowable'—and could help in preventing some future attacks." Below are some of the findings.

- **Targeted violence at schools is rarely impulsive.** Those involved in targeted violence don't just snap. In most incidents, the shooter(s) developed the idea to harm others before the attack. In more than 75 percent of the incidents, the attacker planned the attack either earlier that day or within a few days of the attack. An exception was the Columbine duo, who planned their attack for over a year.

- **More than 50 percent of the shooters had revenge as a motive.** More than 66 percent had multiple reasons for the school attack. Being a victim of bullying was commonly mentioned as a reason.

- **Many attackers communicated with others about their grievances prior to the attack.** In more than 75 percent of the cases, the attacker told someone—in most cases, a friend, classmate, or sibling—before the attack. Distinguishing between a vague threat and a firm intent to harm someone is a job for professionals trained in this area and not a judgment to be made by a parent, teacher, friend, or sibling.

- **Although many friends, classmates, and siblings knew about the attackers' ideas and plans before some of the attacks, in most cases they didn't report this knowledge to adults.** As I stated earlier, this "code of silence" has to be broken. Children must learn the difference between snitching to get someone in trouble and telling to prevent violence. Also schools need a mechanism for anonymously reporting dangerous situations (such as a "hotline" phone or an Internet program, such as Report-it.com). Developing a program in school similar to *America's Most Wanted* and recruiting students as the eyes and ears of the school community are imperative.

Surviving a Massacre, Rampage, or Spree Killing

- **There is no accurate or useful profile of the school shooter.**
  The personality and social characteristics of the shooters varied widely.
  - The age of the school killers ranged from 11 to 21. The shooters came from a variety of racial, ethnic, and socioeconomic backgrounds. In about 25 percent of the cases, the attackers were not white. Additionally, the family profile varied greatly, ranging from dysfunctional families to intact families with numerous ties to the community.
  - Shooters had a variety of friendship patterns from socially isolated to popular.
  - The behavioral history of shooters varied greatly from "no observed behavioral problems" to multiple behavioral problems ranging from reprimands to expulsion.
  - The academic performance of the shooters ranged from failing to excellent, and few of the shooters demonstrated any marked change in academic performance, friendship status, interest in school, or disciplinary actions at school prior to their attacks. This is in stark contrast to the behavior of substance abusers or suicide victims, which clearly shows a decline in academic performance.
  - Fewer than 33 percent of the attackers had histories of drug or alcohol abuse.
  - Few of the attackers had been diagnosed with any mental disorder *before* the incident. This isn't surprising since the latest research indicated 15 million teens suffer from some form of mental illness, and it goes largely untreated and undiagnosed.

- **Most attackers had previously used guns and had access to them.** More than 50 percent of the attackers had a history of gun use, although most didn't exhibit a "fascination" with weapons or explosives. In 66 percent of the cases, the shooters were able to get the weapons used in the attack from their own home or that of a relative; in some cases, they were gifts from their parents.

Spree Killings in Schools

Access to guns among students is common. Because of this easy access, "safe gun storage" is a critical issue.

- **Most shooting incidents were not resolved by law enforcement intervention.** More than 50 percent of the attacks ended before law enforcement could intervene. Of all the school rampages studied, in only three cases did law enforcement personnel discharge their weapons. In contrast to the Columbine High School massacre, which lasted more than three hours, 50 percent of the incidents lasted 20 minutes or less. A 5- to 7-minute window was average for school shootings. During that time, either the attacker was stopped by school staff or fellow students, or ended it on his own.

- **In many cases, other students were involved in some capacity.** In 66 percent of the cases, the attacker acted alone. In 50 percent of the cases, the attacker was influenced or encouraged by others. The following is a true story. A student shared his idea with two friends about bringing a gun to school to appear tough so other students would stop pestering him. His friends convinced him that bringing the gun was not enough; he had to shoot someone to make the others leave him alone. Several days later, he took a shotgun to school and killed two students and injured two others. In another true story, when a "hit list" of students to be killed was issued, some students waited on the steps to watch those on the list get shot. The fact that others knew about both of these incidents in advance contradicts the assumption that all shooters are loners and that they just snap.

- **In 75 percent of the incidents, the attacker had engaged in behavior that caused others (e.g., school officials, police, or fellow students) to be concerned about him.** In 50 percent of the cases, the attacker had come to the attention of more than one person. Actions that alarmed others included the shooter's efforts to get a gun, threatening stories or poems written by him, or alarming talk with friends. So for those who are trained to recognize them, there are red flags that signal when someone is embarking on a dangerous path.

- **In well over 75 percent of the incidents, the attacker had difficulty coping with a major change to a significant relationship, or a change in status.** This could include a divorce between parents, the breakup with a girlfriend, a fight with a close friend, or the loss of status with peers. It could also include personal failure. Some people have difficulty dealing with any type of adversity (I refer to them as *fragile people*). They are on the edge of overt violence, such as damaging property, hurting others, hurting themselves, or all three. Nearly 75 percent of the attackers either threatened to kill themselves, made suicidal gestures, or attempted to kill themselves. More than 50 percent of the attackers had a history of feeling extremely depressed or desperate.

Based on these findings, the Secret Service recommended that a fact-based approach, focusing on a student's behavior or actions rather than a trait-based approach, might be more productive in preventing school violence. In spite of the Secret Service finding that we can't predict with any degree of accuracy who might be a prospective shooter, this doesn't mean that we should do nothing. We will never stop all school shootings, but we can prevent some.

NOTE: I have a couple of problems with the way the study was defined. Only 37 school shootings between 1974 and 2000? That number seems very low. Maybe it was because NTAC specifically dealt with "spree shootings" and neglected other forms of violence in schools. Also the Secret Service did not include shootings related to gang or drug activity or to interpersonal or relationship disputes that occurred at schools. Not including all shootings, stabbings, fights, and riots gives the impression that our schools are "safe."

The following statistics on school-related deaths, shootings, and violence for the 2005–2006 school year by National School Safety and

Spree Killings in Schools

Security Services, Inc., in Cleveland, Ohio, show that this isn't true.

- There were seven school spree shootings during the 2005–2006 school year.
- There were 27 deaths from shooting, 15 from suicide, and four murder-suicides.
- The number of nonlethal shooting incidents totaled 85.

Plus, there were 238 higher-profile crimes, acts of violence, and crisis incidents for that same year. These included gang-related threats and assaults, stabbings, bombs brought to school, and hostage situations, any of which could have easily turned into a spree killing.

Because "targeted violence" is relatively rare, educators seem to think it will not happen in their school, and this study might encourage that misconception. One school safety "expert" was quoted in *Education Week* (October 11, 2006) as saying, "We shouldn't be overly concerned about school shootings because taking into account the number of schools in the country and the spree shootings, the chance of it happening in a school is once in 12,000 years." In addition to being misleading, this minimizes the many other forms of school violence, overt and covert, that undermine academic performance and create physical and psychological problems for students and staff.

ADULT VIOLENCE AT SCHOOLS

School violence isn't confined to student-centered acts. Other potential problems include noncustodial parents trying to snatch students from school and abusive spouses following their partners to work. (Of course, domestic violence is often at the root of spree killings in other locations as well.) Schools should have preventive measures in place to monitor the behavior of parents on school premises as well as that of students.

Finally, school personnel can also be emotionally disturbed or mentally ill, or they can harbor resentments against their supervisors or colleagues. One such example occurred at California State University,

Surviving a Massacre, Rampage, or Spree Killing

Fullerton, in 1976. A custodian at the school library, Edward Charles Allaway, killed seven people and wounded two others before fleeing the scene and latter turning himself in. He had a history of mental illness and was diagnosed after the killings as a paranoid schizophrenic.

A more recent example happened at the University of Alabama, Huntsville, on February 12, 2010. Dr. Amy Bishop, 45, a Harvard-trained neuroscientist who was teaching biology at the Alabama university, was upset about not receiving tenure. At a biology faculty meeting she opened fire on 12 of her colleagues, killing three and wounding three others. The meeting had been going on for about an hour when Bishop stood up, pulled a gun out of her purse, and began shooting people down one side of the table. The others dove under the table for cover. At one point Bishop followed one professor, with whom she had worked and discussed coathoring grant proposals, out of the room and into the hallway, pointed the gun at her, and pulled the trigger. The gun jammed, which allowed the would-be victim to hurry back into the room and close the door. The survivors locked and barricaded the door with the table and a refrigerator, and called 911. One survivor estimated that the shooting rampage lasted about 20 seconds. After her arrest, Bishop's husband reported that Bishop had begun practicing at a local firing range in the days before the shootings. A look into her background revealed that when she was 21, Bishop had shot and killed her brother, but the death was ruled accidental. Later while she was at Harvard, she and her husband were questioned in a case where a colleague, who she suspected was going to give her doctoral thesis a negative review, received two pipe bombs in the mail. No charges were ever filed. This Bishop case clearly reinforces the idea that there are many fragile people out there, and they come from a broad spectrum of the population. This is another rare case where the killer was female.

These incidents happened at universities, but they could just as easily happen at the K-12 level. Schools have to be especially careful whom they employ. Thorough background checks should be required for all employees, from teachers to aides to custodial staff.

PART II

FORMULATING A PLAN OF ACTION

CHAPTER 4

UNDERSTANDING STRESS AND SURVIVAL

The effects of stress on the body will greatly determine the outcome of any survival situation. It is important to understand your body's response to stress so that you can understand the resulting changes in your body and how they impact your survival. There are a number of books that discuss the body's "fight-or-flight" response mechanism to a threat in detail, so I am going to provide only an overview here.

Nature provides us with some basic responses when we are under intense stress. These fight-or-flight responses evolved from prehistoric times and are not always relevant in today's complex and complicated world. What helped prehistoric man run away from a predator armed with a club might not work against an automatic weapon. In fact, that response could get you killed today.

Running is a basic fight-or-flight response. However, knowing which way to run (e.g., running away from the shooter vs. running perpendicular to him) could make the difference between life and death. Once one person begins to run, it triggers others to do the same. Unfortunately, following others might not be the best choice. This is similar to the stampede effect seen in buffalo, cattle, and other herd animals—it can get you trampled, and it allows the killer to concentrate his gunfire in one direction instead of having to disperse it.

Surviving a Massacre, Rampage, or Spree Killing

Your best option is to modify or substitute, if possible, your natural reactions with a more appropriate plan for the specific situation, and this involves training.

Massacres or rampage shootings elicit a *flinch response* from those who are in the kill zone; at greater distances, a less stressful response might result. (It is also known as an *alarm reaction* or a *startle response*, and all these terms can be used interchangeably.) The flinch response is the body's reaction to an unexpected stimulus, such as a loud noise, quick movement near the head, or a flash of light.

From forensics, we know the flinch response is fast. Tony Blauer, CEO of Blauer Tactical Confrontation Management Systems, is a leader in the field of the flinch response and has spent more than 20 years researching and testing its effects on combat (*Law & Order,* October 2003). Much of the following information on the flinch response comes from his work. Blauer describes the flinch response as a reflexive action that will bypass the cognitive systems if the stimulus is strong enough. It is hard-wired into the body's nervous system and cannot be shut off. However, through training it can be incorporated with muscle-memory training. This is important for anyone training in combat, whether a martial artist, soldier, or law enforcement professional. I recommend that anyone concerned about personal safety should check out Blauer's system (www.tonyblauer. com). (More on the importance of incorporating the flinch response into your self-defense plan appears at the end of this chapter.)

Hypervigilance is the heightened state of awareness accompanied by exaggerated behaviors; its purpose is to detect threats. When exposed to a traumatizing experience, such as gunfire or an explosion, some individuals develop an intensified arousal, where they freeze and scan the environment for other threats. This hypervigilance can be seen in video clips taken during the bombing of the 1996 Summer Olympics in Atlanta. After the trauma is over, most people have a heightened startle response. This is evident in students in schools where shootings have occurred, and they are excellent candidates for overreacting in a future attack. For example, I noted in Chapter 3 how students at the University of Central Arkansas were so nervous the day after the murders on campus that the sight of police rushing across campus caused some to panic. People who are "jumpy" suffer from an elevated flinch response. In prehistoric times, this might have been a good thing; it may not be today.

HOW STRESS CHANGES THE BODY

Most of the time, the parasympathetic nervous system (PSNS, sometimes referred to as the "rest and digest" system) controls the normal bodily functions of breathing, heart rate, blood pressure, digestion, and other processes. When a sudden threat occurs, the body instinctively tries to move away from the danger. This is the body's sympathetic nervous system (SNS) kicking in (i.e., the fight-or-flight reaction). This overall emergency response is sometimes referred to as the *general adaptation syndrome.* It takes from three to seven seconds for the chemicals released from the glands (e.g., adrenaline, epinephrine, and endorphins) to be moved around the body in the blood and effect changes. This results in changes all over the body (researchers have identified as many as 144 psycho-physiological changes that occur when the SNS kicks in; these are discussed below).

Conversely, in some people, the SNS's response might result in fainting or remaining frozen in place. This is sometimes referred to as the "fright-or-freeze gene." According to researchers at the University of Colorado and the University of New York at Albany, as much as 15 percent of the population may be genetically predisposed to freeze under high levels of stress. While there may be some survival value in such a response, it is not a great trait for pilots, soldiers, or police officers. Freezing is the crudest form of submissive behavior and acts as a calming agent on more aggressive individuals. While this works relatively well in the animal world (by not moving, animals make themselves less attractive to predators), it is not as effective with human predators. However, in certain situations, playing dead might be the smartest reaction (playing dead as a tactic for survival is discussed in detail in Chapter 7).

Physical Changes

Understanding the physical changes that occur in the body when it feels threatened is important because a sudden attack forces the body to operate under less-than-ideal combat situations. Stress causes the following changes in the body's organs and systems.

Heart and Circulatory System

Heart rate and blood pressure spike when a threat is detected. The heart races to infuse the brain and major muscles involved in fight or flight with both fuel and oxygen. Blood vessels that supply the brain and major muscles open to allow maximum blood flow, while those supplying blood to nonessential organs and tissues shut down.

One apparent sign of this blood flow is visible on the face. A red face is a sign that someone is excited but not yet ready for combat. While this is part of "ritualistic combat" intended to make the person more ferocious looking, he may also become more aggressive, unreasonable, and unpredictable. If you can't verbally calm down the person, you should get out of there if you can. It is likely you need to calm down as well, since coming face-to-face with someone who is excited and aggressive will often create the same response in you. When the aggressor's face turns white, blood has been shifted to major muscles for fight-or-flight, and action will follow immediately.

Lungs

Bronchioles, the small air tubes in the lungs, dilate, allowing for the intake of more oxygen. The person could experience trouble breathing (i.e., hyperventilation).

Adrenal Medulla

Adrenaline and noradrenaline flood the bloodstream, causing an increase in blood sugar and constriction of some "unnecessary" blood vessels. This way blood can channel to fight-or-flight muscles. As stated earlier, it takes about five to seven seconds for adrenaline and other secreted stress-response chemicals to make their way around the body and take effect.

Liver

The liver begins to break down glycogen into sugar for instant energy to maintain the heightened metabolic rate.

Spleen

The spleen contracts and pumps white blood cells and platelets in preparation for possible physical injury. In the event of bleeding, this action speeds up coagulation of the blood to stem blood loss.

Bladder and Colon

The bladder and colon prepare to void their contents in preparation for violent action and possible injury. The sphincters that control elimination from these organs relax, resulting in possible urination or defecation.

Hair

The hair stands on end (piloerection). This reaction may not be very visible in people today, but you can feel it when your SNS is kicking in. We've all had that "feeling" when we were around someone who was creepy or in a situation that was frightening. This reaction is still visible in some animals when they are agitated.

Stomach and Gastrointestinal Tract

Vessels constrict to divert blood away from digestive functions to major muscles for fighting or fleeing. This is one reason athletes don't eat a big meal before a competition. The food will just sit there.

Sweating

In preparation for fight or flight, the body's cooling system kicks in. The body has a narrow temperature range, and even as little as a six-degree increase can have serious consequences. Therefore, evaporation of water from the skin's surface will help cool the body down.

Unlike sweating elsewhere in the body, sweaty palms are triggered by a mental stimulus, such as fear, and aren't associated with cooling of the body. The sweat glands of the palms are connected to the ridges in the hand associated with grasping things, such as prehistoric man grabbing and securely holding a club. Excessive sweating can make the hands slippery and cause you to drop something or lose a grip on someone's hand or arm.

Pupil Dilation
The pupil, the center dark area in the iris, dilates (expands) when the SNS takes over. This widening is a survival response from prehistoric times and allows the eye to take in more visual information.

Mental Changes
When the SNS is activated, creative thought is diminished, making it very difficult to come up with a new plan of action. This is not the time to make choices or decisions. Your natural decision-making ability shrinks, and more primitive responses take over. The need for action surpasses the need for deep thought. This is where proper training should kick in. Training prompts your body to move quickly, initiate a desirable plan, and recognize cues that should trigger an appropriate response. Without training, some preprogrammed natural responses will likely take over, such as panic running or flinching. In that case, luck is about all that you can hope for.

Among the other changes in your mental skills are the following:

- Poor concentration—The ability to concentrate is also reduced, which relates to diminished thought capability.
- Tachypsychia (distortion of time)—Sometimes events appear to be speeded up or slowed down, and it's hard to tell how much time has passed.

Understanding Stress and Survival

- Fear—When a person is under attack, fear will kick in to some degree. In some cases, and with some people, it can be overwhelming to the point where they can't function and might even freeze.
- Negative thoughts—Sometimes bad thoughts (e.g., "I am going to die") will distract the victim from taking necessary action.

THREAT AROUSAL

As you can see below, threat arousal has its positive and negative effects. It is important to know both. Overarousal seems to magnify the negative effects. Through focused training, it is possible to increase the positive effects and minimize the negative aspects of the fight-or-flight response, thus maximizing your survival odds.

Positive Effects

- Heart rate increases and pumps blood to vital body parts, i.e., brain and major muscle groups.

- Body is psyched (or pumped) for combat.

- Arousal makes us stronger for short periods. Afterwards, exhaustion usually follows.

- You become wide awake. There is nothing like a good scare to wake you up instantly. This sometimes happens to drivers after they almost fall asleep on the road.

- The release of endorphins reduces your feeling of pain. Often people who have been shot or stabbed or have broken a bone don't even feel it at the time at all.

- Blood coagulates faster to speed blood clotting.

Surviving a Massacre, Rampage, or Spree Killing

- Pupils dilate to take in as much information as possible.

- Your body wants to live, so it will do everything possible to survive. This desire is stronger in some people than others.

- Blood sugar levels soar to fuel your muscles. The liver and muscles change glycogen into a soluble form that will go to the large muscle groups and the brain. This makes you faster and stronger.

- Sweating keeps the body cool.

Negative Effects

- Excessive heart rate can adversely affect fine and complex motor skills. There is definitely a correlation between heart rate and performance, and it can be positive or negative based on genetics, illness, physical condition, and other factors. If the heart rate is too low, the body is slow to get into the fight-or-flight mode. If the heart rate is too elevated, the body becomes overstressed and functions poorly, making it difficult to think clearly and perform fine and complex motor skills. There is debate about the exact heart-rate numbers at which performance is affected positively or negatively.

- Hypervigilance can cause you to freeze and become incapable of reacting. This could result from your lack of confidence in your ability to control the threat. Proper training will increase confidence in your ability to survive and mitigate this reaction.

- Tunnel vision allows you to concentrate exclusively on the threat and block out all other distractions. Unfortunately, there might be more than one threat (e.g., multiple shooters in different locations), and when tunnel vision kicks in, it is almost impossible to focus on all of them. It also affects depth perception. Can tunnel vision be prevented? Not easily. One suggestion is tactical breathing, which is explained on the next page.

- As the pupils dilate to take in information, you lose the ability to focus on things at close range. From a shooting perspective, it would be impossible to see the sights of a gun, which makes aiming impossible. Tactically, this would suggest using point-and-shoot or laser sights rather than your regular gun sights. Once your pupils have dilated, even if you bring your stress under control, it takes a full second for your pupils to go from a dilated profile to a constricted profile, so that you can then focus on your front sights. One second can be an eternity since most gunfights are over in two seconds or less.

- Auditory exclusion functions for the ears like tunnel vision does for the eyes—it allows you to shut out sounds that don't have relevance to the threat. However, sometimes important sounds are missed as well. This can be especially problematic when dealing with multiple attackers or shooters.

- As discussed above, you may experience a loss of decision-making or reasoning skills, especially if you haven't trained specifically for such a scenario. Impulsive or irrational behavior might occur.

- Movement could become clumsy, which is often exacerbated by poor timing. Hand dexterity and coordination suffer, and fine and complex motor skills deteriorate.

- Light-headedness, dizziness, and nausea can occur.

- Depending on a number of risk factors (e.g., age, health issues, fitness level, and coping skills), the stress caused by a traumatic event (especially a spree killer) can cause a heart attack or stroke, which can be fatal.

Surviving a Massacre, Rampage, or Spree Killing

NOT EVERYONE RESPONDS TO
THREATS IN THE SAME WAY

"It is not the *danger* we fear; it is the *fear* of danger."
— Tony Blauer

Threats affect people differently. A threat that strikes fear in the heart of one person may only provoke anxiety in another person or no reaction at all. The difference lies in the individual's perception of danger and the confidence he has in his ability to handle the situation. A boxer might be very confident in stand-up confrontations but lose poise when taken to the ground by a grappler. Realistic training increases physical abilities, mental discipline, and confidence. It creates a "warrior" mind-set.

Tactical Breathing
When stressed to the limit, police and military personnel use tactical (or controlled) breathing to decrease their heart rates. Done right, tactical breathing can reduce heart rate by 20 beats per minute and restore scanning ability from a state of tunnel vision. However, learning to do so takes time, and it is not advised when the person is in the open and already under attack. It is frequently used before going into combat situations or after taking cover and planning the next move.

The breathing exercise is often referred to as 3 x 3 x 3. The three-step action is performed as follows: breathe in through the nose for three seconds, hold for three seconds, and then exhale deeply through the mouth for three seconds. For maximum benefit, this should be repeated three times.

Responding to Surprise
There is no question that being caught by surprise puts you at a great disadvantage. This is why I stress the importance of mental alertness in Chapter 6. If you are taken by surprise, however, the flinch response may help you to cope.

Understanding Stress and Survival

The flinch response, discussed earlier in this chapter, is a protective mechanism that is activated when a potentially dangerous stimulus is introduced too quickly and without warning. For the flinch response to activate, it must be triggered by one of the body's visual, auditory, tactile, or olfactory sense receptors. These stimuli will bypass a trained response and trigger the flinch response. It is a built-in, genetically programmed, highly reliable (but not infallible) defense response that everyone has, regardless of previous training. It might enable you to survive a surprise attack and still be able to continue the fight.

This response is unconsciously triggered by the amygdala, located in the rear of the brain, which connects directly into the brainstem. This is where the majority of our instinctual reflex responses to danger are stored and includes the changes that occur in the body to prepare it for fight or flight. The main job of the flinch response is to protect the brain.

The flinch response doesn't always help you survive a surprise attack. A successful ambush might not trigger the response in time for you to take action. The flinch response might fail if "presumed compliance" comes into play. Presumed compliance is when someone assumes that no threat exists and compliance is automatic. Making such an assumption—and being wrong—can catch you totally unaware of a dangerous situation. This might cause you to turn your back on a dangerous person and put yourself at great risk. The flinch response could even be detrimental to you. If you are approached from the blind side with a gun trained on you and either the clicking sound of the gun or a visual cue triggers the flinch response in you, your quick movement might trigger a similar response in the shooter, prompting him to accidentally fire—if that wasn't already his intention.

This genetic system isn't infallible. In certain studies when subjects were shown photos of different "unfriendly" facial expressions, the pictures triggered an increased amygdalic response (fight-or-flight response). However, a nice-looking, friendly face didn't activate this response. Some killers who are attractive use the "friendly con" to lure their victims into danger.

Surviving a Massacre, Rampage, or Spree Killing

Cue-Response Training

To survive an attack, two things are critical: threat recognition/processing time and correct response selection. This is referred to as *cue-response training*. The goal is to suppress the flinch response and replace it with a trained response. This process utilizes the unconscious mind to recognize the threat and provide the appropriate action. This requires a lot of training. I often tell students that under stress, the conscious mind isn't reliable; the unconscious mind is far more dependable. The responses in the unconscious mind are either genetically programmed (i.e., the flinch response) or the result of proper training. If you are caught by surprise, it is virtually impossible to prevent the flinch response from being triggered; therefore, you must build surprise scenarios into your training. The only way to prevent the flinch response from taking over is by being alert and paying attention when in public.

Of paramount importance to your survival is the speed with which you recognize a threat and respond to it. Tying cue-response training into the flinch response is helpful in improving speed. Also, it is important that your response be applicable to all kinds of threats. Having a different response for each threat would require a huge number of techniques and tactics, which would be impossible to master and maintain. As an example, a similar defense response can be used to defend against an overhand attack regardless of whether the attack involves a stick, chain, or machete. Instead of trying to create a different defense against each weapon, you might only need a slight modification of the initial movement. Many qualified combat instructors (e.g., martial arts, law enforcement, or military) can assist interested parties in making these adjustments. Most experienced combat instructors recognize the importance of the KISS (Keep it simple, stupid) principle. Having too many responses for every situation complicates the response, slows down reaction time, and requires much more training time to become competent.

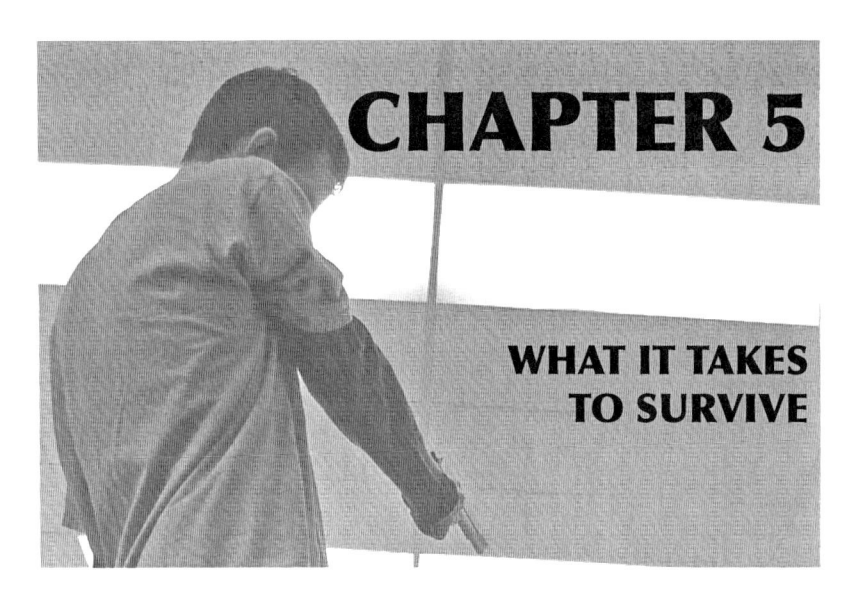

CHAPTER 5

WHAT IT TAKES TO SURVIVE

In a moment's time, civil order can devolve into chaos, as is most certainly the case in a shooting spree. Will you be prepared? The following comment from Michael Rayburn, adjunct instructor at the Smith & Wesson Academy and a top police defensive-tactics instructor, was directed to the law enforcement community, but it is applicable to civilians as well: "The bottom line here is: Don't rely on other people . . . to keep you safe on the street. Your survival is your responsibility, no one else's."

Some folks believe it is not necessary to waste their time training because others will protect them in an emergency. Follow this policy at your own peril. There is too much reliance on police and other emergency service professionals, who can only be in so many places at one time. As you can see from the stories in this book, officers usually arrive at the scene when the rampage is already in progress or after it is over. Often, this is too late to help those at the scene.

I always stress the importance of self-responsibility in my safety seminars for the public, but becoming self-reliant takes training. The purpose of this book is to enhance that training. I hope you will pick up some ideas and strategies for improving your safety. If you think you know everything you need to know now, you are mistaken. Criminal and terrorist tactics are changing constantly; being prepared is an ongoing job. Use whatever learning tools are at your disposal, including newspapers, books, TV, websites, and other sources to improve your safety preparation. I have learned a great deal from the stories told by survivors of rampages. From them you can learn both what some people did wrong and what others did right to help them survive.

ARE YOU A WARRIOR OR A SHEEP?

By their very nature, people fall into either the warrior or sheep category, according to Lt. Col. David Grossman, the director of the Warrior Science Group and the author of the seminal book *On Killing.* Being a warrior allows you some options that won't even occur to "sheep." Sheep will inherently select running away, hiding, freezing, or avoiding direct contact with a shooter, whereas warriors might decide to physically engage the shooter if the opportunity presents itself. I believe the stress of the situation or the need to protect one's family and loved ones might bring out the "latent" warrior in some people.

FIGHT FOR YOUR LIFE

In developing a safety plan, it is important to understand the force matrix. The amount of force an individual is legally allowed to use in a given situation to protect himself or his family is governed by the use-of-force continuum. Using excessive force in public could actually get you into trouble if its use is unjustified. If the situation is not life-or-death but still requires action on your part, keep the following force levels in mind:

- Level 1 is the lowest level of force. It uses personal presence (body language) and verbal communication to resolve conflict.

- Level 2 uses low-level hand techniques. These include escort and restraining techniques and low-level wristlocks and joint locks.

What It Takes to Survive

- Level 3 escalates into hard reactionary techniques, including striking techniques, chemical agents, and cuffing.

- Level 4 includes multiple applications of hard techniques, which might be the use of "nonlethal weapons," including pepper spray chemicals, baton, or Taser.

- Level 5 is the use of deadly physical force.

Law enforcement can stay one step ahead of the perpetrator; you can't. You must legally justify the level of force you use, or face the possibility of legal action. *Just remember, in the middle of a killing spree, you are justified in the use of deadly force. Do what you have to do.*

THE NATURE OF SPREE KILLINGS

They Happen Quickly

Most rampage killings don't last long. Police or other first responders typically arrive fairly quickly, but school shootings average only five to seven minutes and are often over before police can arrive. Other public shootings (e.g., mall, office, church) last longer on average but are still relatively short. The shooter wants to do as much damage as possible in the time he has, so you must do whatever you can do to stay alive during those few minutes until the killing stops.

Spontaneous vs. Nonspontaneous Assaults

In a spontaneous or surprise assault, you get no warning. Does this make the situation more life threatening? You bet. You must act immediately and hope it is not too late. This often means going from totally clueless to defense mode in milliseconds. This isn't the way to survive. It is better to remain alert so you can reduce or eliminate totally spontaneous attacks. With training, you can learn to see a situation developing and establish a plan of action. As discussed earlier, if you are taken by surprise, your flinch response might enable you to survive the first few milliseconds and give you enough time to implement a plan. Once the attack begins, it is essential to initiate your plan immediately. Instinctive action (or trial and error) is better than nothing, but as soon as possible you want your training to kick in.

THE LEARNING CURVE

If you expect your self-defense plan to kick in at crucial times, understanding the learning curve is essential. There are four stages of the learning curve: unconscious incompetence, conscious incompetence, conscious competence, and unconscious competence.

Unconscious Incompetence

A beginner knows little or nothing about a subject (in this case, self-defense), so instructors must assume total ignorance on the part of a new student. This is what Bruce Lee referred to as the "empty cup." Instructors must discern which students are motivated and the attributes they bring to the table. Without motivation, the work ethic will be lacking. If you don't have a strong work ethic, you won't put in the time and effort necessary to develop critical survival skills.

Conscious Incompetence

With proper instruction and leadership, you will recognize the need to improve and practice. At this stage, you recognize how little you know and realize the need to expand your knowledge, skill, and expertise.

Conscious Competence

Here you realize that you know what to do and how to do it. However, you still have to think about it, which is fine for noncombat jobs and low-stress situations. Unfortunately, this level relies on the conscious mind, which is very unreliable during emergencies. With time and quality practice, you will progress to the final stage.

What It Takes to Survive

Unconscious Competence

This level of achievement is essential if you expect the proper responses to be available during stressful encounters. At this stage, the unconscious mind has taken over the process of mental alertness and combat defense, and is working 24/7. Well, maybe not while you sleep, but when you're awake, it should be working. This is the combat-ready mode, and it is the goal of self-defense training. In a life-or-death situation, you might not get a second chance. So, you must get it right the first time.

If you actually survive an encounter, afterward you likely won't even remember what you did. Everything runs on autopilot, which means the unconscious mind takes over. This is the martial arts concept of *mushin*, or acting without thinking. In high-stress combat situations, anything less is just not good enough. Level four is the stage of awareness most wild animals maintain, regardless of what activities they are engaged in. If this system fails them, they will be dinner for some predator.

THE IMPORTANCE OF TRAINING

"When facing a life-and-death situation, preparation is an important companion."

—Jeff Arnsperger, police instructor

Is your training sufficient? Reading this book—even more than once—won't be enough to overcome the panic of a surprise attack. At best, it will bring you to level three of conscious competence. To succeed, you must operate in unconscious competence, and this can only be accomplished through training.

Competency training for stress requires perfect practice in order for you to become proficient. When I was younger, I was constantly told that "practice makes perfect." Later in life, I learned that practice makes permanent, whether it is good or bad, and only perfect practice makes perfect. Having a qualified instructor train you is the best option.

Surviving a Massacre, Rampage, or Spree Killing

According to some experts, 4,000 to 10,000 repetitions are required to make a tactic instinctive so that it can be performed under stress. Without this level of repetition, most people would be incapable of physically defending themselves against a person with a weapon. Most people either seriously underestimate how much training is required or don't have the work ethic to practice until they become proficient. You sometimes hear stories about an 80-year-old woman who disarms a robber and beats him silly with her pocketbook. These instances do occur, but they are the exceptions to the rule.

For those who say they don't have the time or energy to do all this training, I urge you to reevaluate your priorities. If you really don't have the time, there is another option that will allow you to improve your chances some. A number of TV programs entitled "wildest this or that" feature a variety of riots, shootings, and attacks. Watching these shows could be helpful to the trained and untrained alike. By watching these clips, you train your eye to see the visual cues that could signal trouble. There are almost always some warning signs when trouble is on the way (Chapter 6 will give you some ideas and specifics as to what to look for).

Role Playing

Role playing should be an important part of your training program. It is a great way to sharpen your mind and increase the speed with which you make decisions. As you go through your daily routine, pick out someone and imagine that person to be a shooter in a rampage scenario. Assess your environment and quickly determine what your course of action should be. Practice this often in various scenarios. In time, you will find that you will be making faster and smarter choices.

Counter-for-Counter Principle

Martial artists, law enforcement officers, and military professionals practice this tactic during their training sessions. Essentially, you must train so that you can adapt for changes in an adversary's plans or actions. This is sometimes referred to as "switching to plan B." In addition, sometimes you have to change plans not because your adversary switched but because your initial plan isn't working. So you switch to plan B and continue as long as feedback indicates that it is working. You might have to go to plan C or D or even fall back to plan A if circumstances change. This is why you must remain as calm and rational as humanly possible throughout the ordeal.

Scientific Method

Another methodology for acquiring proper survival skills during training is through the scientific method. This is better than trial and error, but most experts in the field don't advise it. The scientific method begins with identifying a problem and finding workable options to solve it. After collecting as much information as possible from the experts, sit down and formulate a plan that you can execute. I highly recommend that you work with a competent instructor to train you in the skills you will need to carry out your plan.

One of my concerns is that there are often a few too many "experts" out there. I always find out the credentials and background of anyone whose advice I may have to rely on. I want to understand the basic principles or science on which their plan is based. I then look to see if their advice fits into my overall plan.

Practicing Preplanned Strategies

You should have multiple plans to respond to a shooting incident. This is called *preprogramming*. Studies have shown that developing preplanned strategies can reduce response time from 150 milliseconds to 20 milliseconds. This is very important since, as we have seen, even a millisecond delay can prove fatal.

Training Rules

Training the unconscious mind to recognize the threat and trigger the appropriate response is essential. The following training rules will help you achieve this.

Surviving a Massacre, Rampage, or Spree Killing

1. Drill the skills and techniques until they become second nature and part of long-term memory.
2. Minimize solutions and cut the BS. Too many programmed solutions will result in valuable time lost while the brain tries to select the correct response. More isn't always better.
3. Train for realistic situations (specificity of training). Training in gym clothes instead of the clothing you would likely be wearing in the street isn't recommended. Nor is training barefoot if you would be wearing shoes in the street.
4. During training, you want to minimize injuries as much as possible, without compromising realism. After all, having a broken arm or torn ACL would limit how you could respond to a real-life attack. So use safety equipment, but don't get used to techniques that require safety equipment that won't be available in real-life situations. For example, wearing protective gloves to train isn't advised since in a real altercation you'd be using bare hands. You need to toughen up your hands and other striking weapons (e.g., knees, elbows, feet) in training so they aren't injured on contact. For example, punching an opponent in the head with your bare hands could result in broken fingers—not something that would serve you well in a fight for your life.

Countering Survival Instincts

Some experts suggest that no amount of training is going to override a person's survival instincts and that it is smarter to follow these instincts. This presumes that following these instincts is the best course of action. Today's threats are different from the threats on which many of these instinctive responses were based. The following examples illustrate this.

When a woman is being followed, it is instinctive for her to run home, a place of known safety. In prehistoric times, this would mean returning to the cave and the tribe for protection. However, today, you should be very concerned about letting a stalker know where you live. You probably don't have a tribe there to protect you! Training should override this instinct to run to the nest. It is smarter these days to go to a public place for refuge—e.g., a police station, fire station, or hospital.

When the shooting or explosives starts, people often instinctively freeze first for a moment or two to determine the location of the threat. I can't overemphasize that this delay could be the difference between living and dying. Unfortunately, we are hard-wired to identify the source of the threat before acting. Develop a plan and train so that your automatic response is a planned one.

Another instinctive response is to run away from the threat in a straight line, without any thought of cover. Let me tell you, it isn't easy to outrun a bullet. Of course, running is always a valid option to consider when trying to escape a shooter, but learn how to do it the right way. Chapter 7 explains when to run, how to run, and when to seek cover or concealment.

SOME TRUTHS ABOUT WINNING CONFRONTATIONS

Winning a life-or-death battle takes a combination of knowledge, skills, alertness, and training. The following will give you a bit of insight into what you need to do to prepare yourself for a life-or-death confrontation.

Confidence

You can't buy confidence. Confidence is something that has to be earned through practice and achievement. Having confidence in your ability to handle a situation will keep your stress level from going through the roof and allow you to function at peak performance levels. It is common today to find some educators trying to "give" confidence to young people. I have even noticed in many martial arts schools that almost everyone is being promoted regardless of skill level. This is a way to make people feel better about themselves (or keep paying tuition), but confidence can't be conveyed by someone else. It must be earned the old-fashioned way: through hard work.

Endurance

Endurance can't be faked. As with confidence, a lot of hard work goes into the development of endurance. In this case, it involves performing appropriate exercises over and over. While many confrontations—especially killing sprees—are over quickly, you can't count on that. During a confrontation, stress will deplete oxygen at a rapid rate and cause exhaustion, even in runners or trained athletes. And if an opportunity arises for you to try to escape, this will definitely require endurance. This is where training comes in.

What Does It Take to Win?

Winning takes will and absolute commitment to achieve. At the risk of sounding like a broken record: *winning requires a commitment to quality training*. As the late Coach Bear Bryant of the University of Alabama football program observed: "The will to win compares little with the will to prepare to win." Winning requires the ability to go to battle at a moment's notice. Paul Roemer, a former FBI trainer, said of training, "We are the products or victims of our training." I always add, "Or lack of training."

This is a classic case where what we don't know *can* hurt us. Combat situations require knowledge of the dynamics of the battlefield and of the enemy. Do you know who or what you are dealing with? Emotionally disturbed people and terrorists function differently and have different goals. Spree killers usually end their attacks quickly, but terrorists may drag out the killings. It is also important to know your own strengths and weaknesses. Tony Blauer asks the following question to those he trains, "Are there any rules in street combat?" To which he answers: "Only those you bring along." You must understand that there are no rules in a killing spree; don't hamstring yourself by bringing along your own. Anyone who trains in sport fighting or boxing won't adapt quickly or at all to street survival.

WHAT IF YOU AREN'T ALONE?

As if developing a plan of action for yourself isn't difficult enough, imagine having to develop a plan for family members or friends who are with you when an attack occurs. For example, what if you decide to take the family to the Fourth of July parade. We already know that parades and other crowded public events often attract criminal elements, including emotionally disturbed people, gangs, and other troublemakers looking for easy marks or multiple targets. Add to that the consumption of alcohol or use of drugs, and a pleasant family outing could turn into a nightmare.

A shooting during a 2009 Mardi Gras parade in New Orleans illustrates this perfectly. Two gunmen, aged 18 and 19, fired into a crowd, striking seven people, including a toddler, all innocent bystanders. The situation quickly turned into chaos, with people ducking and running everywhere. Fortunately, police were stationed nearby, and they were able to apprehend the shooters quickly. Fortunately, no one died, but the shooters intended to kill as many as they could.

What can we learn from this example? We seldom hear or read about the dangers posed by parades, theme parks, rock concerts, and sporting events. This isn't a coincidence. These events bring in big money to cities, communities, and businesses, and no one wants to jeopardize that revenue by publicizing the risks.

If you and your family or friends decide to go to a crowded event, inform each person in your party ahead of time that, when you give directions or orders, they should be followed immediately and without question. Make each person agree to abide by this. While this sounds simple, when people are stressed or panicked, they have a difficult time following directions. Make a plan before you go; when you arrive, point out to the others where the exits, security, first aid, and safe places are located.

Surviving a Massacre, Rampage, or Spree Killing

CONCLUSION

Executing a plan gives you a better chance of surviving than relying on random action. While it might work under some circumstances, random action isn't your best bet. Whatever action you select, act instantly. Every second you delay makes you (or those in your charge) more likely to be injured or killed. You have to train properly to get the mind-set, skills, confidence, and endurance to implement the right plan (or series of plans) instantaneously. This takes hard work and dedication.

CHAPTER 6

RECOGNIZING DANGER

During prehistoric times, man's survival depended on his paying attention to his surroundings at all times. You would think that over the millennia, we would have gotten pretty good at recognizing danger and assessing risks, wouldn't you? But we haven't. This might be in part because the risks are always changing or are masked, so we don't recognize them. Another reason is a trait that scientists refer to as *optimism bias*. This is the notion that "it won't happen to me." I often hear this from educators when discussing school killings. Thinking that it can't happen to you is a disincentive to being prepared. This misguided belief has caused us to allow our survival skills to atrophy.

While most members of society have become very complacent, others have become more violent and have sharpened their predatory skills. With modern weapons, even one person is capable of doing tremendous damage. "Technology has made each individual potentially more of a menace to society, here and around the world," says James Pinkerton, a noted newspaper columnist. Between rapid-fire automatic weapons and explosives of all types, the average person is capable of wreaking tremendous havoc on an unsuspecting crowd. While crowds are a deterrent to some criminals, they are an attraction for the spree killer.

Surviving a Massacre, Rampage, or Spree Killing

Most people are in such a hurry these days that they allow their minds to be preoccupied by things they need to do and places they need or want to go, often putting themselves at risk. Their attention is easily distracted by elaborate window displays, fancy cars, or headphones plugged into their ears. In the past few years, a new and more pervasive diversion has emerged: the cell phone. People walk the streets with this device glued to their ears, completely clueless as to their surroundings or possible threats.

Although we no longer have to worry about the saber-toothed cat, today's predators are even more dangerous. Evil is always on the prowl looking for an inattentive person. This chapter will show you how to be more alert so that you recognize the signs of potential danger.

GETTING REAL ABOUT RISK

An often-neglected area of survival planning is risk management. This involves reviewing the dangers of an activity or location in advance. Almost anything we do has potential hazards, but we often trade off these dangers because of the reward or excitement promised.

Many people are incapable of identifying any potential threats during their activities (either routine or special) because they either don't have the training or are too caught up in the moment to be concerned. Sporting events are a great example. They are exciting to attend, but many championships in recent years have resulted in riots afterward—and it doesn't always matter whether the home team wins or loses. For example, in 2008 violent "celebratory riots" erupted in Boston after the Celtics won the NBA Championship and in Philadelphia after the Phillies won the World Series. Fortunately, no one was killed or seriously injured in those riots, but 13 people were trampled to death when a riot broke out during a World Cup–qualifying match in Harare, Zimbabwe, in July 2000.

Spring break is another activity that can be dangerous. Young people (or their parents) pay little attention to the activities that can put all, males and females alike, at risk. The use of copious amounts of drugs and alcohol diminishes attentiveness and the ability to recognize real danger. In addition, it interferes with people's survival skills and their ability to defend themselves.

People often misjudge risk. They think they can either control a situation or get the subject to cooperate with them (presumed compliance). Whenever you go to crowded places, don't assume that you can control the actions of others. Individuals react reasonably most of the time, but when they don't, you are often caught by surprise if you have made naive assumptions.

It is important to assess your tolerance for risk. Some people enjoy the thrill of jumping out of a plane; others don't. Some people get a thrill when going into a high-risk location or situation, while others would be frightened out of their minds. There are documented cases of people deliberately going to watch a riot firsthand. Yes, you heard me right. During the terrorist attack in Mumbai, India, a crowd formed when the police cordoned off and trapped one or two terrorists in the hotel. The crowd scattered quickly when the terrorists opened fire. What were the police or the spectators thinking? That there was going to be a parade? Don't let risk-taking put you or your family in extreme danger.

Last, it is important to continue to monitor your environment for risks and dangers even after you think the danger has passed because things can change in an instant. What does this mean? Stay alert! Continue reading, and I will suggest ways of doing that.

LEVELS OF ALERTNESS

One of the ways to achieve mental alertness is using a program developed by the late Jeff Cooper, called the Color Code System of Mental Alertness. Cooper's system is well known by law enforcement personnel and civilians, and can be found in many books and articles. Here, I have summarized it and adapted it for use by the general public.

The Color Code System is divided into five colors, signifying varying degrees of alertness: white, yellow, orange, red, and black.

Surviving a Massacre, Rampage, or Spree Killing

- Color Code White—the lowest level of mental alertness. At this level a person is totally unaware of what is going on around him. Most of us go through life at this level, without even realizing it or recognizing how dangerous it could be.

- Color Code Yellow—the level you should try to be in most of the time. You are aware of your surroundings and use your senses (principally your eyes and ears) to take in information all around you. This level is often referred to as *scanning*. An important note: scanning allows you to watch the full range of your peripheral field, as opposed to tunnel vision, discussed earlier, which zeroes in on a specific threat. While at this level, make it a habit to watch for exits and escape routes, especially when in a crowded place.

- Color Code Orange—the level you assume when something disturbing or alarming catches your eye or ear. This could be a shadow suddenly appearing, footsteps heard from behind, or body language or behavior that suggests danger. You immediately evaluate the seriousness of the danger and respond. In addition to using your conscious mind, learn to trust your instincts and your unconscious mind, which combines the best of both worlds. This way, you have nature's warning system working with what you have learned in life. This doubles your chances of success.

- Color Code Red—the level to which you escalate if you recognize a threat. Immediately, you formulate a plan of action and begin to implement it. Which plan you select will be based on the threat information you perceive. Unless you *respond* quickly in Color Code Red, you will be *reacting* to some type of assault or threat.

- Color Code Black—the level you're in when under direct assault. At this level, you must rely on your training and combat skills for survival.

Recognizing Danger

I can't stress enough the importance of programming the Color Code System into your unconscious mind. The element of surprise is such a critical factor in combat situations that even highly trained individuals can lose encounters when caught off guard. It is important to avoid being taken by surprise for a number of reasons. First, being surprised might prevent you from getting out of a situation before it turns violent. Second, it takes five to seven seconds for adrenaline to kick in and get your body ready for combat. The "bad guy" knows this and will strike suddenly, without giving you any chance to resist. Your aim is to have a plan of action kick in while you are in Color Code Orange or Red. If you find yourself in Color Code Black without a plan, it might not matter what combat skills you have because you might not have a chance to activate them. Maintaining the proper levels of awareness is the equivalent of military groups posting sentries to alert the group to danger.

SAFETY IN GROUPS?

Is it safer to be in a group or alone? Here again, we can learn from animal behavior. Why do zebras, giraffes, and other animals hang out in groups? There are more eyes, ears, and noses to detect danger. You might think that there is safety in groups for people as well. For example, when traveling in a group, it isn't necessary for each individual to maintain the same level of alertness as is needed when you are alone. This would be true if you were concerned about being targeted by a criminal looking for a vulnerable or defenseless individual. Unfortunately, this isn't the case with a spree killer, who generally targets groups. But the good news about being in a group is that there should be more eyes and ears looking out for danger, right? Unfortunately, people in a group are often so distracted by conversation that they aren't alert to any risks. Being in a group has a mixed benefit. But whether you are in a group or alone, always maintain the proper level of alertness.

Surviving a Massacre, Rampage, or Spree Killing

ASSESSING DANGER

Physical Appearance

Most of us base our first impressions of people on their physical appearance, which can be deceptive. What a person looks like can trigger a sense of urgency or presumed safety. For example, while physical appearance might warn us that someone is dangerous, a skillful criminal can hide his intentions with appropriate clothing and body language. Ted Bundy used his good looks and smooth talk (and fake cast) to get close to and then kill dozens of young women.

Relying heavily on physical appearance is risky, but it can provide the earliest warning signs. Is the subject clean or dirty? Is he well groomed or unkempt? Being dirty or unkempt could be a sign of mental illness. Is his clothing appropriate for the day, season, or social circumstance? A long raincoat or trench coat would be inappropriate during hot weather and could conceal a weapon. The Kauhajoki school shooting in Finland is a case in point. On September 23, 2008, Matti Juhani Saari—masked, dressed in black, and carrying a large bag—entered the school and started firing into a classroom where students were taking an exam, killing 10 (*Newsday*, September 24, 2008). How many red flags should have caught someone's eye: the mask, the black clothing, the bag, his walk? Plus, Saari had posted disturbing clips on YouTube, showing his fascination with firearms and the Columbine killers, postings of which the authorities were unaware.

Another physical indicator of danger is a person's demeanor or mood. Does the subject appear angry, hostile, depressed, apathetic, or euphoric for no apparent reason? Are the emotions appropriate to the circumstances? Is the person laughing inappropriately? Is there any evidence of rapid or extreme mood swings? Is there a lack of expression—e.g., is the face devoid of any emotion, or does he have a "thousand-mile stare"? Eyewitnesses to spree shootings have sometimes described the shooters as staring right through the people to whom they spoke.

Prejudices sometimes influence our assessment of people. For ex-

Recognizing Danger

ample, some people register negative impressions of fat, handicapped, ethnic, or religious people, regardless of their potential for harm. Since the 9/11 attacks, for example, Muslims in the United States are often mistrusted and suspected of being terrorists. But someone in a priest's or nun's garb probably would be judged harmless. Age can also be a misleading indicator, of both the young and old. At first, a child or an elderly person might seem innocent and get us to drop our guard, but that could be dangerous. There is no minimum or maximum age limit for mass murderers—in this book we have examples ranging from 11 to 88. The same is true for gender. Though most spree killers are male, being female doesn't mean that a person isn't dangerous.

Recognizing Suspicious Behavior

When evaluating potential risks, we are constantly being told to watch out for suspicious behavior. But what constitutes suspicious behavior? Nobody ever tells us that. With today's bizarre dress and behavior, how can you tell the difference between what's harmless, what's weird, and what's dangerous? Sometimes you can't.

A dangerous person doesn't necessarily exhibit bizarre behavior, and a person who acts strangely isn't necessarily dangerous. Humans are capable of manipulating and controlling body language, and many do. Some dangerous people can control their behavior to appear nonthreatening, neutral, or even submissive, lulling you into a false sense of security, which could turn deadly.

Still, there are warning signs that the trained eye should pick up. Being able to detect subtle clues in behavior or gestures is a skill that members of law enforcement agencies, security personnel, or those trained in reading body language acquire over time and rely on to spot dangerous people. Since this is a learned skill, we can acquire it as well.

Suspicious behavior can mean several things. First, any "strange" behavior should be suspicious. This would include pacing nervously, acting tense or jumpy, or looking around furtively or repeatedly. Someone carrying a concealed weapon might constantly touch his pockets, waistline, backpack, or package.

Surviving a Massacre, Rampage, or Spree Killing

People acting disorderly should be considered potentially dangerous. Also pay careful attention to anyone who appears to be disguising his appearance: wearing a wig, hat, fake beard or mustache, or sunglasses; or having a tan line where a beard might have just been shaved off. Be suspicious of someone who suddenly shows up to work in an area where no work is usually being done, or of someone wearing a uniform who is where he shouldn't be (especially if the uniform is generic or not quite right). A stranger in an area where most people are known to each other might signal trouble. Seeing someone taking pictures, videotaping, or using a stopwatch, even in unrestricted areas, should alert you. If you see the same individual repeatedly hanging around the same place, report your observations to security.

Of course, it's not just people's behavior that can be suspicious, but also objects. Be on guard if you spot an object where it shouldn't be: bags or backpacks left unattended or a strange vehicle in an inappropriate location. If you see someone dropping a package and running off, contact the appropriate authorities. If you find weapons stashed in public places (such as cleaning closets or trash receptacles), get security right away. *Warning:* Never touch or move a suspicious package because moving it, if it is a bomb, could trigger it. Don't use a cell phone or radio in the area of the suspect package because that also might trigger it. Never confront or try to detain anyone thought to have placed the package. Stay away and warn others to stay clear. This is a job for professionals.

Mental State

Mental health professionals use a technique called "orientation x 3" to help assess whether a person is emotionally disturbed and/or dangerous. This simply means determining if the person can recognize person, place, and time:

1. Does he know who he is?
2. Does he know where he is?
3. Can he identify the day, month, and current year correctly?

Recognizing Danger

After ascertaining these answers, other questions have to be answered. Does the person express suicidal or homicidal thoughts? Is he making overt or covert threats to himself or others? Does he display delusional thinking (e.g., does he think he is god or a fictitious character)? Does he express irrational thinking (e.g., being followed, bullied, or persecuted, which could signal paranoia)? Does he demonstrate erratic behavior? When speaking with him, does he exhibit a "flight of ideas" (i.e., the conversation jumps from topic to topic and is difficult to follow)? Does he exhibit hallucinatory episodes, which could result from alcohol- or drug-induced psychosis?

Unless you are a mental health professional, you can't accurately or instantly diagnose mental illness. But if a person doesn't know who or where he is, or doesn't know the current day or year, and you can answer "yes" to any of the additional questions above, then he is disturbed and possibly dangerous. It's time for you to execute your plan of action, whether that's leaving immediately or calling the professionals.

Speech

Speech reveals a lot about a person's state of mind or mental health. Volume often reflects mood. Angry people are loud and boisterous, whereas depressed people tend to be subdued. Angry people generally speak faster. Changes in speech from fast and loud to low and slow often indicate mood swings. A change in voice, as if the person is having a conversation with someone else or hearing voices, is also a cause for alarm.

Social Interaction

How is the subject interacting with others? Does he appear frightened, provocative, cooperative or uncooperative, responsive or nonresponsive? Frightened people can be especially dangerous and unpredictable when they suddenly find themselves surrounded by others, whom they may perceive as threats.

Surviving a Massacre, Rampage, or Spree Killing

Subject's History

Of course, knowledge of someone's past history is one of the best predictors of future actions, but this isn't always possible. If the person is someone you work with or goes to your school or church, then maybe you are familiar with his history. Does he suffer from some form of mental illness? Is he on medication? Has he been arrested for violence in the past? Has he spent time in prison? Is he a gang member? Has he been known to carry a weapon? Is he hotheaded? Is he an ex-boyfriend, former employee, or disgruntled customer?

In school or the workplace, this information might be known, but it isn't always shared with teachers, coworkers, or supervisors. In the workplace, seeing a fired employee hanging around is a definite red flag, and police should be notified immediately. Having an ex-boyfriend or spouse show up at your house or follow you should trigger an alarm. Call the cops. Stalking is far more common than most people realize and should be taken very seriously. A recent report from *Security on Campus* (Winter/Spring 2009) suggested that 20 percent of college women are stalked or harassed by a former boyfriend. There have been numerous cases where even a restraining order wasn't enough to protect the victim from being hurt or killed.

Gut Feelings

The final category to consider when assessing a person's danger potential is your "gut feeling." It can often alert you that something is wrong with a person or situation even when nothing appears amiss. As man has become more "civilized," he has developed extremely sophisticated mechanisms for rationalizing away these gut feelings. Over time, he has turned off these protective instincts—and amazingly still survived. However, with the state of the world today, it is wise to start listening to these gut feelings more closely.

DETECTING A CONCEALED WEAPON

All the spree killers in this book had to bring their weapons to the scene somehow. They either stashed the weapons in advance, hid them under their clothing, or, as is common with rampage killers, stored them in a gym bag or carryall. A trained person can usually recognize when someone is carrying a concealed weapon.

The three basic requirements for bad guys (or good guys for that matter) carrying weapons in public are concealment, accessibility, and retention. These three criteria seriously limit the locations where weapons can be concealed and yet still be accessible.

Clothing

Clothing can be very effective in hiding weapons. Any clothing seen as out of place should catch your attention. Keep in mind that inappropriate clothing can sometimes be easily explained. For example, people near airports, train stations, and bus stations might appear to be inappropriately attired for Miami, but their clothing was fine when they left Minneapolis that morning. Also, homeless people often wear all the clothing they own all the time, but they aren't necessarily carrying a concealed weapon.

The most well-known example of using clothing to conceal a weapon is wearing a long coat to hide a rifle or shotgun, but there are other cues. Long shirts with their tails hanging out of pants can be either a fashion statement or a cover-up for a concealed weapon. Some schools now require students to keep their shirts tucked into their pants to eliminate the waistband as a handgun-stashing location. If you see someone in a sweatshirt with a hood who is not wearing the hood up in bad weather, be wary: this might indicate a concealed weapon (gang members sometimes use the hood to hide handguns). Watch for an unnatural sag or protrusion of a jacket or pocket. Guns are heavy and will cause jacket or pockets to droop. In extremely cold weather, a coat might be left unfastened to allow quick access to concealed weapons. A coat draped over an arm in bad weather instead of on the person might conceal a weapon in the hand. Also leaving one hand ungloved in cold weather might be so the person can quickly grab and use a weapon. A limp or stiff walk might indicate that the person is carrying a concealed rifle in his pant leg.

Keep an eye out for people carrying such items as oversized purses, knapsacks, soft briefcases, gym bags, folded-over newspapers, or paper bags that seem out of place. Some commercial fanny packs are designed with a quick-open Velcro strip to enable the wearer quick access to a gun. Even regular fanny packs can conceal all types of weapons.

Male offenders tend to carry handguns in the middle torso area, and most don't use holsters. Unholstered handguns tend to shift, which can provide an important clue because the perpetrator will frequently touch the weapon to ensure that it is still hidden and accessible. This is especially noticeable after a person changes body position (e.g., standing up, coming downstairs, or getting out of a vehicle). If a person is running, his actions may be even more pronounced.

Because bad guys think differently, they use ingenious ways to hide weapons that wouldn't be acceptable to the rest of us, such as in a baby seat or stroller or in a bra. So be creative in evaluating possible hiding places for weapons.

CONCLUSION

Remaining alert is your first line of defense for any self-defense situation. Learn the levels of alertness and always remain at the appropriate level for the setting. Train yourself to look for warning signs in a person's appearance, demeanor, and behavior. Learn when to trust your first impressions and when to take a closer look at a person who is slightly "wrong." Know where weapons are commonly concealed and the telltale clues that should make you suspicious.

Don't be misled by an angelic face. The jails are full of them. A violent offender can come in any size, shape, age, ethnicity, or gender. You must be on constant alert for threats and ways to avoid dangerous situations.

CHAPTER 7

SURVIVAL TIPS, STRATEGIES, AND TACTICS

The strategies and tactics in this chapter are based in part on what has worked (or not) in past killing sprees. What is the right plan? Is there a "magic bullet"? Unfortunately, no. Each circumstance is different: the players, the setting, the weapons, the motivations, the response from law enforcement. Plus, there are so many factors involved in each encounter that the circumstances and environment will eliminate one or more choices immediately. You must constantly reevaluate what you are doing and be prepared to choose the option that is best under the specific circumstances.

Before getting into specific tips, strategies, and tactics, let's review what we have learned so far. Everyone has built-in survival responses—among them, hypervigilance, freezing, running, panicking, and tunnel vision. Under certain conditions, one or more of these responses may kick in. Each one offers some degree of protection—and danger. Can you learn to overcome these instinctive responses or at least minimize the risk they present? Yes. How can you change your behavior to enhance your chances of survival? Analyze the problem, come up with viable options, learn from the mistakes of others, and then practice, practice, practice. Remember, perfect practice makes perfect responses. The best tip I can give you right now is not to wait until the shooting starts to come up with a plan of action. By that time, you have missed many opportunities to avoid a bad situation. Prevention/avoidance is the best defense. Being alert goes a long way toward avoiding being caught in a rampage or spree shooting.

One of the most important things that you can do as part of your training is make sure that you are physically fit. While there are numerous stories of people accomplishing incredible feats of strength during an emergency, you need to be fit if you have to run for your life or take on an armed assailant. Running even a short distance, 20 feet or so, is difficult if you haven't been running in your training. Even though the body will automatically respond when the sympathetic nervous system kicks in to release adrenaline, an unfit body might break down when it is most needed. It is like pushing a machine beyond its capabilities and expecting it to perform well. Combining stress and physical exertion with an unfit body doesn't result in top performance.

Additionally, even a fairly fit body without proper nutrition can't be expected to perform at its best. In an emergency, you want optimum performance. Proper nutrition, including adequate carbohydrates and hydration, is essential for your body to function efficiently. This is especially true if the situation is prolonged.

• • •

OK, you know how stress affects your body, both negatively and positively. You know what it takes to survive and have developed a plan of action. You have trained realistically and repeatedly so that you can override your instinctive responses and choose the best option for the circumstances. You are in the best shape of your life: mentally alert, physically fit, and nutritionally balanced. You're ready for whatever. Then it happens. You're at the mall with your family, and a spree shooter opens fire. What do you do? Freeze, run, hide, attack? Of course, escaping is always the best option, but it may not be safe. The following are some options if escape is impossible.

Survival Tips, Strategies, and Tactics

FREEZING

Freezing happens when you're caught by surprise and experience hypervigilance, during which you try to locate the danger. But some individuals can't get out of the freezing phase. Because predators are usually attracted to movement, freezing does offer a limited amount of protection under certain circumstances. However, in the case of spree shooters, I don't see freezing as a very successful strategy.

Playing Dead

Playing dead is a variation of freezing, but unlike freezing, playing dead is an intentional strategy. You consciously decide to lie motionless on the ground, looking as if you were dead. When might this strategy be attempted? If you are too far away from reliable cover or wounded so that you can't run, dropping down and playing dead might be the only reasonable option. But remember, if you do decide to play dead, your body position must convince the gunman that you are dead. You must remain absolutely still and silent. This might work because spree shooters are pressured by time and focus more on those trying to escape. If you can fool the killer long enough for him to either leave the area in search of more victims, prepare to engage police, or commit suicide, you might survive. *But not always.* The Virginia Tech killer revisited a couple of rooms, searching for survivors and shooting those he found still alive in the head to make sure they were dead.

RUNNING

Running away from danger is one of the most commonly programmed responses. But before deciding to run, there are four important questions you must ask yourself. What kind of shoes am I wearing, sneakers or high heels? What kind of physical condition am I in? Do I have an injury or condition that will prevent me from running? What about the people with me—can they run? These are all important factors to consider before taking off. If running is your choice, the next question is where to run?

Is getting distance from the shooter the most important goal? I don't think so. Even if there is some distance between you and the shooter, you might still be in the kill zone. So it is more important to get out of the line of fire and out of sight than far away. This means learning to move tactically: improving your position with effective movement, which will decrease your chances of being a target. Running down a long hallway isn't a great idea unless you are faster than a speeding bullet—*which you aren't.*

I often hear experts suggest running in a zigzag pattern to prevent the shooter from getting a good shot. You had better be in good shape to do this because it requires a lot of energy. If you elect to run, select the quickest direction to get out of view. If possible, use cover or concealment to conceal your escape as you run in a perpendicular fashion. A good example would be a doorway, exit, car, shrubbery, wall, or building. If you run laterally to the shooter, he will have to make adjustments with his weapon to get you in his sights. It takes a shooter about two seconds to align his sites and fire at someone running laterally. It is much easier to aim and shoot at someone running straight down a hallway or an open field.

The urge to run sometimes triggers the panic running of others. This often results in people rushing in all directions, and not necessarily to a safer place. If you are in a large, tight group, the tendency is to go with the group. Resist this instinct. This could result in your being crushed or trampled. Once the stampeding starts, the group will not slow down just because someone falls.

Tueller Drill

There is no such thing as a safe distance—there is only how much time do you have? The Tueller drill is a self-defense exercise created by Sergeant Dennis Tueller of the Salt Lake City Police Department that effectively defines what the danger zone is for close-quarter combat. Tueller originally devised it to help a person armed with a holstered pistol (or unarmed) defeat an assailant armed with an edged weapon. It turns out the lessons learned from this drill can be used to help someone run away from a shooter as well. Tueller determined that the average person can cover 21 feet in 1.5 seconds. So run almost anywhere that would get you out of the shooter's field of vision within the 1.5- to 2-second time frame.

HIDING

If you can't escape, then hiding might be your best option. Reports from actual rampage shootings show that the gunmen usually do only cursory searches for people hiding when mass casualties are their goal. If a shooter enters a room and doesn't see a target at first glance, the odds are high that he will move on until he sees someone in plain sight. If he comes to a door that is locked, he will most likely move on. That is, unless he saw people go in there; then he might take the time to get in. The above applies to random shootings, when the shooter has no specific targets. If you are the specific target and he thinks you are hiding in a room, he will try his best to get in to get to you.

If you believe the gunman didn't see you enter the room, get in the closet or jump behind the counter. Conceal yourself, remain quiet and still, and listen carefully. In this instance, your ears might well be your primary source of information. While waiting, look around for something to throw at the shooter's head to distract him if you decide to rush him. If you can't find anything, your shoe will work. But remember that movement creates noise, so be very careful not to give away your position by squirming or shifting as you remove your shoe or reach for an object to throw.

Sobbing or heavy breathing could attract attention; use the tactical breathing exercise explained in Chapter 4. If you are carrying a cell phone or pager, turn it off. If it rings (or even vibrates on silent mode and might startle you and trigger a reaction), it could reveal your position to the shooter.

Surviving a Massacre, Rampage, or Spree Killing

During a spree shooting at the Pinelake Health and Rehab nursing home in Carthage, North Carolina, on March 29, 2009, the estranged wife of shooter Robert Stewart survived by hiding in a bathroom inside a locked-down area for Alzheimer patients. Stewart killed seven Alzheimer patients, aged 78 to 98, and one nurse as he went room to room hunting for his wife. One very important note here is that the shooter was unaware of his target's location; she had been reassigned to the new ward just that morning, unbeknown to Stewart. When he learned that his wife was in the Alzheimer ward, Stewart headed there but was stopped by a police officer who arrived about one minute after the shooting started. The officer and Stewart shot each other in the hallway, but both survived.

One important note: don't remain in your hiding space if the opportunity to escape presents itself in case the shooter comes back to check for survivors.

Cover vs. Concealment

Two common forms of hiding are cover and concealment, but there is a big difference between the two. Concealment simply makes you invisible (which significantly reduces your chances of being shot), whereas cover makes you invisible and offers some protection from the bullets. If the shooter sees you hide, the bullets could go right through whatever conceals you. The public's perception of what is safe to hide behind, based on movies and TV shows, is very distorted and mostly inaccurate. Don't think because you are behind a door, wall, or even a car that you are safe from the bullets. If you take refuge behind a vehicle, get behind the engine block; it has the best chance of stopping or deflecting bullets.

When you are behind cover or concealment, resist the temptation to look out to check on the shooter. You risk revealing your position and possibly even getting shot. If you must peek, keep it very short, one to two seconds at most, and peek low instead of at eye level. A low peek is far safer because it is less expected.

Survival Tips, Strategies, and Tactics

Lockdowns and Barricades

Lockdowns and barricades take hiding to the next level. If you take refuge in a room, lock the door behind you if possible. (This is especially critical if there is no other escape route from the room and the gunman knows you are in there.) Turn off the lights and lower the blinds or draw the curtains to prevent anyone from seeing you from the outside. Then barricade the room. Move furniture or other items in front of the door to block it. A barricade works better on an inward-opening door but will at least provide an obstacle on an outward-opening door for the shooter to have to navigate. This might slow him down or even trip him up.

While the shooter is distracted getting through the obstacles, this might be your best opportunity to go on the offensive. Your main goal is to convince him that it's not worth the effort to pursue you. Look for an object that is light enough to bash him in the head with if he attempts to come through the door. Another possibility is a door ambush, which is explained in the next segment.

Because lockdowns are simple to execute with minimal training, schools, corporations, and institutions have made them the number-one option for siege situations. And lockdowns often work because most shootings are over in a matter of minutes, before the lockdown can be breeched. Therefore, anything to delay a shooter from reaching targets is beneficial. The problem is that you may overlook an opportunity to flee if you focus too narrowly on the lockdown.

ATTEMPTING AN AMBUSH

Making the decision to ambush a shooter should not be taken lightly. Planning and some serious skills are needed to have any chance of success. Any ambush requires the element of surprise. Plus, there are a number of other variables to consider: Are there multiple shooters? What type of weapons does the killer have (e.g., guns, knives, bombs)? Are you in the shooter's field of vision? Does he appear to be under the influence of drugs or alcohol? You might not know all the answers, but you should gather all the information you can before attempting an ambush.

You should execute the ambush when the shooter turns a corner or can be approached from a blind side. You might play dead and use the element of surprise on him. The door ambush gives you perhaps the greatest chance of success, and having a number of elements in place will increase its effectiveness.

Door Ambush

If you find you can't create a meaningful barricade or lockdown, then consider the door ambush. Door ambushes have been used successfully in a variety of situations involving terrorists, rampage shooters, hostage situations, riots, and multiple attackers.

The door ambush has a good chance of succeeding if the shooter has to fight his way through a barricade. He is quite vulnerable as he struggles to move the door and material out of his way. Again, the element of surprise is crucial here. But how can you count on surprise if the shooter knows you're in there? The shooter is probably not really expecting resistance, and he doesn't know exactly where you are.

If there is more than one shooter, the door ambush allows you to focus on one shooter at a time. The doorway acts as a choke point, prohibiting more than one person from entering at a time. Once you have neutralized the lead person, take the fight to the others as soon as possible. It might mean stripping the weapon from the first person and using it on the other assailants, or retreating to a more defensible position. You might use the first person through the door as a shield or shove him backward into the others to buy you time to escape. As always, the situation and terrain will dictate proper tactics. Improvised tactics might include using furniture as a barricade, throwing ashes from an ashtray in the attacker's eyes, having intense light coming from behind you to blind the attacker, getting to higher ground, or funneling entrance into a room.

Here is how to execute a door ambush, step-by-step.

Survival Tips, Strategies, and Tactics

- Enter the room and locate an improvised weapon, something with substance but that can be swung quickly.

- Turn off the lights and close any shades or curtains that allow light into the room. Anytime a person goes from light to dark or dark to light, it takes the pupils of the eyes about four seconds to adjust.

- Activate any machines in the room (e.g., copier, computer, television, fan, radio) to distract the shooter if he enters. The noise or movement will focus his attention elsewhere while you hide.

- If possible, position yourself on the side of the doorway *away* from the hinges, where the door swings open. Since behind the door is the most likely place to hide, most intruders will look there first. Stay within an imaginary 45-degree angle between the wall and the center of the room.

- Make sure he can't see any part of your body or weapon. Stay tight to the wall. Be careful when leaning against the wall to maintain noise discipline. Touching or rubbing against the wall might produce sounds.

- If the room is dark and the outside is light, as the shooter enters he might flip on the lights; this might be your best chance to attack. If he has a flashlight, you will know where he is looking based on the beam of light.

- When the gunman comes through the doorway, he will encounter some blind spots in the room, and he can't see both hard corners (the right and left corners of the room immediately beyond the entrance) at the same time. The distant corners are "easy corners" because they are in the visual field, provided there is sufficient lighting. (Cops use an entry technique called *slicing the room*, which cuts the room into small segments, but it is slow and time consuming. A spree killer doesn't have that much time before police arrive. He has a choice to either get whoever is in that room quickly or go elsewhere.)

- When the shooter enters, he will assume that his victims are unarmed and unprepared to resist. This will encourage a hasty entrance, which gives you the element of surprise. He might also be under the influence of alcohol or drugs, which further encourages rash behavior.

- Be prepared to clobber the gunman in the head or face with an improvised weapon immediately as he walks through the door. If you have pepper spray, all the better.

- As soon as you strike him in the face, grab for his gun with both hands. As you attempt to disarm him, try to point the gun in a safe direction. If the disarm doesn't work and he pulls the gun back (a natural reaction), shove it into his face. *(Warning: It isn't my intent to teach you how to perform gun disarms here; you can't learn how to do disarms by reading a book or watching a video. Learning how to physically disarm a shooter requires specific training with a qualified instructor and a lot of actual practice.)*

- Not every gunman uses a pistol; some prefer rifles or even shotguns. The rifle might have a sling to keep it secured to the user's body. Different disarming techniques are required for a long gun.

- The shooter's attempts to control his weapon will likely pull you toward him. As this happens, drive your knee into his groin or lower body, and then attempt to strip his weapon away again.

- If your strip is successful and you get the gun, aim center mass and if necessary shoot him.

Survival Tips, Strategies, and Tactics

- Move toward the doorway to engage other hostiles if necessary.

RUSHING THE SHOOTER

If no opportunity for ambush exists, you might have to rush the shooter. Rushing in to engage a gunman in hand-to-hand combat is one of the toughest decisions you will ever have to make. At close range, though, it might be your best choice.

If you are less than 10 feet from the shooter, you are in the kill zone. You have to decide immediately whether to rush and physically engage the shooter. Unless you have trained for such a scenario, it is even harder to decide this under the stress of actual battle. Once again, the information from the Tueller drill applies: at 10 feet or less, it will take you 1 to 1.5 seconds to engage the shooter. If rushing is your best option, here are some tips.

- If possible, avoid rushing from the frontal position, for obvious reasons. Instead approach from anywhere within the shooter's peripheral field of vision.

.
- If you must approach from the front, throw something at the shooter's head to initiate the flinch response in him, which will momentarily disrupt his vision and ability to shoot. If no other object is available, throw your keys, wallet, shoe, gloves, or anything in your pockets.

- If a shooter stops to reload, consider rushing him. In several of the stories in this book, you saw that the spree shooters stopped to reload, so you know this happens. If you are within 10 feet of him, you can probably reach him before he can reload and fire again.

- Once at close range, follow the same assault plan as for the door ambush. After the assault, try to take the shooter facedown to the ground.

Surviving a Massacre, Rampage, or Spree Killing

- If others rush with you to disarm the shooter, use the same procedure to take him to the ground and secure the weapon.

- If approaching the shooter from the rear or side, outside his field of vision, pick up something to smash him in the head. In this case, it might be better not to throw the object, but rather to wait until you are close enough to smash him. However, if the shooter turns toward you, then throwing the object at his face is advised.

Will rushing the shooter work? Here are two examples where lives were saved by rushing the shooter under the appropriate circumstances. The most recent example happened at Deer Creek Middle School, just three miles away from Columbine High School on February 23, 2010. After shooting two students with a high-powered rifle in the school parking lot, the shooter, Bruco Strong Eagle Eastwood, was tackled by math teacher David Benke as he tried to reload. Other school staff helped to restrain the shooter and gain control of his weapon. As a result, no other casualties occurred. The latest information seems to indicate the 32-year-old shooter was emotionally disturbed, if not mentally ill.

As we saw on page 28, the quick action of three passengers on the Long Island Railroad train limited gunman Colin Ferguson's casualties to six dead and 19 wounded when he opened fire on passengers with a 9mm Ruger pistol. Ferguson had an additional 160 rounds and could have killed many more were it not for who rushed him and took him to the ground. As with Eastwood, Ferguson was mentally disturbed.

DEFENDING AGAINST AN EDGED-WEAPON ASSAULT

Though spree killers in this country favor firearms, you must still be prepared for the threat of a bladed weapon. Some rampage killers carry knives as backup weapons, and more people are hurt by edged weapons than firearms every day.

Survival Tips, Strategies, and Tactics

Types of Edged Weapons

Anything with an edge or point is considered an edged weapon. Bladed weapons can be divided into seven categories, based on the method in which the weapon is used: stabbing, slashing, stabbing or slashing, hacking or chopping, throwing or shooting, projectile, and spears, bows, and blowguns. Recognizing how an edged weapon might be used is helpful in coming up with a plan to defend against one.

Stabbing

Stabbing weapons include small knives, scalpels, ice picks, ninja spikes, scissors, pens, pencils, dirks, and shanks. Scissors are one of the most dangerous bladed weapons for two reasons: their slightly triangular shape produces puncture wounds that don't close properly and therefore heal slowly, and they are usually loaded with germs and bacteria. Prompt medical attention is needed to stop the bleeding and prevent infection.

Slashing

Slashing weapons include razors, X-Acto or carpet knives, and some rings and belt buckles. Some street gang members carry single-edge razor blades in their cheeks.

Slashing or Stabbing

Slashing or stabbing weapons include hunting knives, stilettos, Western fighting knives (e.g., Fairbairn-Sykes), and scalpel.

Hacking or Chopping

Hacking or chopping weapons include machetes, cleavers, and axes. A large bowie knife can do it all.

Throwing or Shooting

Throwing or shooting weapons are a mixed bag. Throwing stars and spikes, throwing knives, and axes fall into this category. Throwing stars are probably the most accurate, but they are generally not capable of killing. A throwing knife requires great skill to hit a target and even more skill to hit a moving target. Most skilled knife fighters wouldn't throw their knives.

Projectile

Projectile knives are rather rare but should be considered extremely dangerous at distances of less than 15 feet. Some knives actually shoot low-caliber slugs.

Spears, Bows, and Blowguns

Spears, bows, and blowguns, while not common, are found in some areas and could be dangerous in the hands of someone trained in their use.

Who Uses Edged Weapons?

Many tradesmen carry and use knives for their work. The knife is a very common weapon among mentally ill or emotionally disturbed people. What a disturbed person might lack in skill is often made up for in enthusiasm. There are a number of skilled knifists out there, including kali and arnis/escrima enthusiasts, biker and street gang members, and Western-style knife fighters (military trained). In jails, blades are the weapon of choice (and opportunity), and inmates are often quite skilled in their use.

Protecting Vital Areas

If attacked by an assailant with an edged weapon, you must first act to protect vital areas: wherever arteries and veins are most exposed. Most tend to be buried in muscle, but the ulnar arteries and veins in wrist, femoral arteries in the thighs, and the carotid arteries and jugular veins in the neck are particularly vulnerable.

Cuts through the skin and scalp are generally not that bad; they just look bad because of all the blood. Few people die immediately from a single knife wound. If you die, it is usually from a loss of blood, and, depending on what is cut, exsanguination takes time. Never stop fighting or trying to escape because you are cut.

But if you believe that you will die when you are cut (or shot), you just might. People are more likely to be incapacitated mentally than by the actual damage, and then they stop fighting. Often those who were stabbed thought they were punched and never knew until later that they had been stabbed. You are probably better off if you can't see the wound. The body is amazing when it comes to protecting itself. Blood flow is slowed by autoregulation, swelling of the tissue around the wound, and coagulants released as part of the fight-or-flight response.

Sidestepping vs. Stepping Back

If someone rushes you with a knife, stepping backward buys you no real time. Sidestepping has proven to be far more effective, and timing is crucial in any fight. A determined attacker running at full speed will find it impossible to "turn the corner." However, nothing beats having an obstacle (e.g., a car, wall, post, fence, piece of furniture) between you and the rushing knife wielder.

USING A FLASHLIGHT

You should always carry a small high-intensity flashlight in your pocket because it comes in handy for a lot of things—including blinding the shooter by shining it directly in his eyes. The bright light causes his pupils to constrict, which could give you up to four seconds to either escape or rush him while his eyes are making the necessary adjustment. Four seconds is enough time to cover about 40 feet.

DEFENDING AGAINST EXPLOSIVES

Explosives are used more by terrorists than spree killers, so why include a section on explosives? Because rampage killers may get ideas from terrorists and sometimes do include explosive devices in their arsenals, especially now that information on them is readily available on the Internet.

Responding to a Hand Grenade

Hand grenades are plentiful and found in military operations around the world. A grenade is an extremely dangerous antipersonnel device, which is popular with both terrorists and drug cartels. During a recent shootout between Mexican soldiers and members of a drug cartel, 50 grenades were exploded (*Newsday*, June 8, 2009). Grenades have recently been found among the drug gangs in Texas, and some are beginning to find their way onto the streets. Grenades (likely stolen from military arsenals) are obtainable on the black market. How long before we see someone using a grenade in a mall, airport, school, or train station?

If you are in an attack where a grenade is thrown, try to observe where it lands. You don't want it to roll in your direction, but don't panic if it does. A panicked response won't help at all. To overcome your initial response to run from a grenade, you must practice the following technique. Have someone toss a full can of beans to simulate a grenade at random times so that you begin to develop a conditioned response. Initially, it might be best to practice diving and rolling on mats or a carpeted floor so that you don't hurt yourself until you get the moves down.

Grenades have timers and will usually go off in two to four seconds (it is impossible to tell exactly when they will go off). If you run, you may be struck with fragments or spun through the air by the blast's shock wave. Either dive for cover if it is available or dive to the ground away from the grenade as quickly as possible and lie facedown. Point your legs, with heels together, toward the grenade and your head away from it. The soles of your shoes will act as a shield between your body and any fragments from the explosion. Since fragments radiate outward, at most you would be exposed to those few fragments traveling parallel to the ground. The soles of your shoes, your feet, and legs will act as a shield to absorb any fragments before they penetrate vital organs. Minimizing your body's exposure to flying fragments is only part of the problem. You still have to contend with the shock wave.

To protect the ears, lungs, and upper body, move your elbows against the sides of your rib cage and cover your ears with your hands. In this way, you protect the vital areas in the body, the ears from the shock wave, and the head from flying material. When a grenade explodes, a shock wave expands out from the center of the blast. This high-pressure wave can rupture the eardrums and lungs if you are too close. Holding your hands over the ears reduces outside pressure and minimizes tissue damage. Close your eyes and open your mouth to equalize the outside and inside pressure.

RESPONDING TO POLICE PRESENCE

In the excitement of seeing law enforcement arrive, you might be tempted to run toward the officers. *Don't.* They too are under stress and probably don't know who the killers are or how many there are. If you approach, they might shoot you or physically force you to the ground until they can determine that you aren't a threat. Stay where you are, or do exactly as they instruct you to do. Arguing with or resisting police orders will cause trouble and waste time that can be used to stop the killer. Instead, maintain cover or concealment until the police gain control of the situation and tell you it is safe to come out.

DEALING WITH THE AFTERMATH

Although knowing how to handle the aftermath of a rampage will do nothing to prevent you from experiencing one or to keep you alive during one, it will go a long way toward helping you survive afterward. It is important to understand how a violent event will impact you and those close to you.

A critical incident is any event that has an impact stressful enough to overwhelm normal coping skills. They are typically sudden and powerful, and could be either man-made or natural: rape, murder, abduction, earthquake, flood, and fire. Being caught in a murderous rampage certainly qualifies as a critical incident.

The effect brought on by a critical incident is sometimes referred to as *battle fatigue.* This is often associated with soldiers suffering from what used to be called *shell shock.* In 1980, the American Psychiatric Association formally recognized the civilian version of battle fatigue as post-traumatic stress disorder (PTSD). PTSD can result in physical, emotional, and cognitive reactions. Physical reactions include headaches, sleep disturbances, change in eating habits, decrease in sexual activity, and so forth. Emotional reactions include anxiety, fear, sadness, anger, withdrawal, and in extreme cases suicide. The cognitive reactions could include debilitating flashbacks, nightmares, lack of concentration, and difficulty making decisions and solving problems. Symptoms must last more than 30 days to be officially diagnosed as PTSD.

After seeing these possible symptoms, you can understand why it is so important to follow up with the "critical incident stress debriefing" process. Between 4 and 10 percent of the people experiencing a traumatic incident, if untreated, will suffer PTSD but won't know it until much later. Regardless if it is resolved peacefully or with force, a life-or-death situation can still be traumatizing. Therefore, it is strongly suggested that you seek help within 48 hours to prevent the escalation to PTSD. Be proactive in your treatment; don't wait to see if symptoms appear. It could take years before they do.

The tenth anniversary of Columbine in 2009 found the survivors and their families still in pain. Traumatic events aren't easily forgotten. Here are some suggestions for victims and their friends and family members.

- In the immediate aftermath, the victim should not be left alone.

- Denial is an easy coping mechanism. Look for changes in behavior or attitude as warning signs of denial.

Survival Tips, Strategies, and Tactics

- Learn the signs of physical, emotional, or cognitive reactions and check for symptoms.

- Be aware that PTSD may not appear for quite some time and the symptoms may be sporadic.

- Alcohol and street drugs have no place in the recovery process. They only mask the problem and slow the recovery process. If you are given drugs by your doctor, take them as prescribed and remain under your doctor's care. Do *not* take drugs that have been prescribed for other people.

- Peer and family support is invaluable.

- Close family members and coworkers should be included in the treatment.

- If counseling isn't offered, request it. Don't be macho and say you do not need it. You really can't tell. After 9-11, many police and firefighters suffered serious emotional consequences because, for whatever reason, they did not take advantage of debriefing. Counseling, in addition to the stress debriefing, might be necessary.

- Taking time off for rest and recuperation might be necessary for your physical and emotional recovery.

CHAPTER 8

SUGGESTIONS FOR THE EDUCATIONAL COMMUNITY

"Unthinkable and horrific events have occurred in recent years that have affected this country's first responders in ways previous disasters, whether natural or man-made, cannot compare. September 11, 2001, ushered in the age of terrorism from abroad that shocked Americans by its vicious intensity. April 16, 2007, brought the specter of death looming across the serene setting of a university campus [Virginia Tech] that destroyed the last vestiges of innocence in its wake."

—FBI Law Enforcement Bulletin, May 2009

Professionals in emergency services and law enforcement are trained to act as first responders. What would happen if, for whatever reason, they couldn't get to a school or campus in reasonable time during a shooting spree? Then, teachers and staff would have to fill that role as first responders. How prepared are they to handle a crisis of the magnitude of the Virginia Tech massacre?

While this scenario frightens most people in the educational community, they deny the possibility of such an event happening on their campuses. It has happened before at several schools and campuses, and it will happen again. Maybe on your campus. Everything possible must be done to help prepare the educational community to be ready and able to act. This chapter focuses on the problems facing that community and provides recommendations about what to do.

Marc Fisher, a columnist for the *Washington Post*, wrote an interesting opinion piece in *Newsday*, April 20, 2007, just days after the Virginia Tech shootings, entitled "Eight Years Later, Nothing Has Changed." In the article he asked whether America had learned nothing from the Columbine killings. Apparently not, but the reason might surprise you. U.S. District Judge Lewis Babcock ruled that the information gathered for the trial and other records, including the videos describing the killers' evil plan, must remain sealed for 20 years. Even though lessons from Columbine might help prevent a future killing spree, the judge felt the information might trigger copycat killers. Guess what? It triggered copycat killers anyway, both in the United States and abroad, but law enforcement and educational agencies were prohibited from benefiting from the information.

Here is a case in point: "A Columbine-Type Plot Is Foiled in Kansas and Missouri" (*Education Week*, April 26, 2006). In Missouri, two suburban Kansas City teens were charged with planning a Columbine-style shooting. Trevor Fattig and Sean Amos, both 17, told classmates they planned an assault on Platte County R-3 High School. About 150 miles away in Riverton, Kansas, five students were arrested after posting details on MySpace of their planned attack at Riverton High School. Both plots were scheduled for the seventh anniversary of the 1999 Columbine attack.

The reluctance of the educational community to acknowledge and tackle the problem of school shootings is based on many factors. In some cases, there are legal obstacles to overcome, including privacy laws that prohibit sharing much-needed information about mental health and juvenile criminal records. As to other reasons, I have heard all the excuses administrators give as to why they don't train their staff on this critical issue. The most common reasons are "our hands are tied," "we don't have the funds," "we don't have a problem," and "we don't want to frighten anyone." Hiding behind these flimsy excuses can be costly, in dollars *and* lives.

Suggestions for the Educational Community

LEGAL CONCERNS

Unfortunately, the U.S. Constitution and the judicial system prevent legal intervention until a person actually commits a crime. This might not be the most efficient approach to preventing violence, but it's what we have to work with. Because of a variety of concerns, schools are leery about identifying children who *might* be dangerous. But just see what happens if a student in your school is killed or injured in an attack—the parents will come down on you like a ton of bricks. In nearly every district where there's been a killing, the victims' families have filed lawsuits. School law experts place the average settlement in such cases at $250,000 *(School Principal's Legal Alert)*.

The families of three victims at Columbine sued the principal and other school employees in Jefferson County *(Education Week,* August 2, 2000). The lawsuit alleged that school officials had indicators that Eric Harris and Dylan Klebold were prone to violence but failed to act prior to the shootings. Three lawsuits originally filed against the Jefferson County Sheriff's Department were amended to name the school principal, the school district's security directors, and three teachers by name. Twenty other unnamed school employees were also included in the suit.

On the second anniversary of the Virginia Tech rampage, two families of slain students filed suit against the State of Virginia, Virginia Tech and its counseling center, several top university officials, and a local health agency, citing gross negligence. One of Cho's teachers had recommended counseling for him because of his troubled nature, a fact that was part of the public record. The families sought $10 million in damages. These were the only two families who did not agree to an $11 million settlement with the state. *(Newsday* April 17, 2009.)

Further, the courts are beginning to give the educational community some guidance when it comes to protecting children. According to Chief James McBride, a member of the Ohio Governor's Task Force on Campus Safety, "Federal and state courts are finally giving all of us guidance. . . . In many cases, judges are rendering decisions that suggest campus officials have a significant obligation (if not duty) to 'police' their own facilities in order to adequately protect their 'invitees' and their workforce" (*Law and Order,* June 2009). This should give pause to those administrators who insist on burying their heads in the sand over the issue of school violence.

WHAT EDUCATORS NEED TO DO

It's not rocket science. There are a few things that schools should do that could make a big difference. The following should be top priority for every school district in the country.

Violence-Prevention Training for Everyone

Educators should begin with quality violence-prevention training for everyone, including administrators, teachers, support staff, secretaries, and custodians.

After teaching public school, both junior and senior high, for 33 years, teaching two school safety graduate courses for almost five years, and speaking at more than 40 educational conferences locally and nationally, I feel qualified to evaluate the performance of the educational community when it comes to school safety. If I graded the educational community the way teachers grade children, I would give it between a C and D, and in some cases an F.

I don't mean to imply that there aren't teachers and administrators out there doing a great job providing school security, because there are. Unfortunately, they are in the minority. I know many real school-safety experts, and they share this view. So for those who are doing the right things, God bless; and for those who aren't, shame on you. If that seems a little harsh, it is meant to be. I have never been accused of being politically correct—I say it as I see it.

Schools have a wide variety of violence issues that get more talk than action. Apparently few in higher education think these are important. Here is a chilling example: New York State requires that new

Suggestions for the Educational Community

teachers take a *two-hour* school safety course. Does anyone believe you can learn anything about school safety in two hours that will actually make a difference? Yet, I don't hear the Board of Regents, New York State Education Department, the colleges, school boards associations, teachers unions, school administrators, or any other educational body question this.

In addition to teaching two school-safety graduate courses (90 hours) a number of years ago, I was asked to teach a six-hour block on school safety for a masters in administration program. This was for future deans, principals, and superintendents. The following year, I was asked to come back and teach a two-hour block on school violence for another group of potential administrators. When I questioned the decision to drop the program from six to two hours, I was told, "That is all New York State requires." It gets even better. To qualify to teach the two-hour course, you must complete a six-hour instructor's course. *Six hours?* This is like the blind leading the blind, and it is very scary.

Each state should mandate a minimum of 45 hours of school safety training, which should be offered through the colleges and universities. The instructor should have experience in education *and* violence prevention. Most school districts require staff development and in-service training; these programs should bring in experts on school safety. Administrators often put an educator in charge of violence-prevention training because it is cheaper and easier. Unless this person also has experience dealing with violence, this is ineffective and possibly dangerous. Law enforcement is a great resource, but it cannot do it alone. Cops do not have the knowledge of what educators face on a daily basis.

Teachers will be first on the scene when there is trouble and so must be prepared. They should be trained in body language and verbal communication skills to recognize, prevent, and deescalate dangerous situations when possible. Teachers aren't even trained in what to do about fights, which are an everyday occurrence in many middle and high schools. I would never suggest that a teacher attempt to physically break up a fight, but many have attempted to do so to protect children or preserve discipline. It often results in either injuries to students or staff, or lawsuits.

Report Violence Accurately

Another problem is that many school officials do not report all—or even most—of the violence in their schools. An audit of a dozen New York State schools by the state comptroller's office concerning dropout rates found that many districts underreported dropout numbers by as much as 7 percent. Based on this, how accurate can reports of school violence be? From my experience, underreporting school violence is much more prevalent. First, this information is blocked from leaving the building. Schools are big, and often teachers in the building don't know when a violent event occurs. Anything that gets to the superintendent's office is further filtered or sanitized. No one benefits from this censorship.

Create a Mechanism for Reporting Violence

A mechanism or system must be in place for students, parents, teachers, and other staff to report suspicions or threats of violence made against individuals or the school. A district hotline that allows anonymous tips is one option. Another is to hire a company to set up a website for reporting threats anonymously; an example is Report-It.com, an online tipline service to which schools can subscribe. Whichever option is chosen, schools have to be prepared for crank calls. A trained professional should be assigned to review these calls for follow-up. Confidentiality is essential; if the name of the person reporting the threat is known (it should not be mandatory), it should never be divulged to the student being investigated. This is done in some schools, and it discourages others from reporting.

Connect with Parents

Parents must be part of the plan. Schools should offer programs for parents to identify the same warning signs that are taught to teachers. It might be hard for parents to check on what their children are up to. Some parents feel guilty about checking their child's room, computer, or text messages. Psychologist Peter Langman, author of *Why Kids Kill: Inside the Minds of School Shooters,* advises parents and educators to "think carefully about children's demands for privacy." Parents should want to know their children's friends, where they spend time when they're not at home, and what they do on the Internet and the websites they visit. This is especially vital with teenagers, but I have found this is the time when parents seem the least involved in their children's lives. Just go to a high school PTA meeting and see how few parents of teenagers attend.

Sometimes parents or teachers come across indicators of an attack in the form of drawings, sketches, animation, a video, or a short story. Students will try to explain these away, saying that they were merely "being creative" or fantasizing, or they claim a First Amendment right to say or create whatever they want. Assume that these threats are real until proven otherwise. Law enforcement and mental health professionals should investigate these threats.

Educators should follow through with due process regardless of who is involved. Often children with influential parents (or parents who are teachers) get preferential treatment. For parents, if the school expresses concern about your child, pay attention. They typically have the best interests of the child in mind. Parents too often side with their children and believe anything their kids tell them. Another point Langman stresses in his book is that parents should not lie to protect their children. You are not doing the child a favor, and sooner or later there will be consequences—for the children and the parents. The more you protect children, the harsher the consequences will be in the end.

Punishment is not prevention. Just expelling or suspending a student doesn't change the behavior. In fact, sometimes it makes the child angrier, and we have seen examples of students who were punished or expelled from school returning with weapons on a deadly rampage. Troubled kids need professional help, and the school and their parents should get them that help, as early as possible.

Surviving a Massacre, Rampage, or Spree Killing

Connect with Law Enforcement

Educators around the country are slowly beginning to work more with the law enforcement community. This has to be speeded up. Educators should encourage random school walk-throughs by police officers. The random visits would put potential evil-doers off balance and allow officers to be more familiar with the school layout in case of an emergency.

I have always been an advocate of a professional school resource officer (SRO) in all schools. That presence alone would make many—students and staff alike—feel safer. The SRO would assist in developing a school safety plan, be the liaison with law enforcement, handle difficult and antisocial students, and be on the scene as quickly as possible in the event of a shooting or other act of violence. Michael Dorn, director of Safe Havens, the world's leading nonprofit campus safety organization, says, "I absolutely would not have a child in a middle or high school, college or university without armed personnel."

I am an advocate for a permanent, *professional* police presence in schools, rather than the rent-a-cop security officers usually employed. Many school security officers are poorly trained, out of shape, and not equipped to deal with violent situations. During a visit to one school, I asked the security guard if he was supposed to physically break up fights. He said yes. I then asked if he had been trained in how to break up fights. He said no, that's why he thought I was there. I was *not* there for that purpose. To do that would require police defensive tactics training, which take at least a month of full-time training (40 hours per week).

QUESTIONS FOR SCHOOLS ON CRISIS PLANNING

- **Do you have an existing plan on how to respond to a bomb threat, explosion, shooting, earthquake, hurricane, or other destructive event, and is the plan known to everyone involved?** This plan should be developed with the input from all the departments and agencies that are going to be responding: police, emergency services, fire department, and the entire school staff, not just teachers and administrators. Custodians will play a major role in any catastrophic event.

- **If you don't have such a plan, where should you start?**
  "Many educators are putting too much faith in electronic gadgets and spending too little time on training and planning. . . . Prepared schools will also train all staff," according to Ken Trump, the president of National School Safety and Security Services Consulting in Cleveland (*Education Week*, April 23, 2003).

  You begin by putting together a team of people from the school. This team should include people from all areas, including administrators, teachers, custodian staff, secretaries, nurses, school security staff, guidance staff, aides, and bus drivers. Include people with different areas of expertise and from different locations on campus. They all see building problems differently and will all play a role in the execution of the plan. Students must also be trained to carry out the plan. Otherwise how can they be expected to know what to do and stay calm?

  Then invite a security specialist from either a law enforcement agency or a private security company to do a security analysis of your school. Next, a systematic approach to identifying and correcting security risks should be outlined and implemented. Training must occur on a continuing basis because there is always a turnover in staff and people forget what they don't practice on a regular basis. Keep in mind that an open college campus has very different needs than a public high school or middle school.

- **Do you have the appropriate equipment to contain or mitigate a violent attack?**
  Certain pieces of equipment are critical when dealing with school crises. Intraschool communication is an essential compo-

nent of any security plan. Administrators must be able to communicate with their staff during a crisis, whether they are in the classrooms or moving around the building or grounds.

Many schools now rely on cell phones for mobile communication. Many might be surprised to learn that law enforcement will shut down cell phone signals if they think the attackers are using cell phones to detonate explosives or to communicate with associates on the outside. This is especially so if the authorities suspect terrorism. For example, during the Mumbai attack, terrorists received instructions and real-time updates about the police forces massing against them. Some of the phones the terrorists used were taken from hostages. The intelligence they gained from cell phones made their attack much more effective and deadly. This might not seem to apply to school students, but a lot of teenagers are very technologically savvy and very familiar with how cell phones can be used.

Most schools have an intercom system connecting all classrooms, but in my experience, they don't always work. It is essential that they be made operational. How can a teacher get prompt help in a classroom emergency if not through the intercom? Many schools also use walkie-talkies with their security teams.

Another communication device that can be used to provide campus information is electronic message boards. They should be strategically placed in the entrances to all buildings, in the cafeteria, and on every floor. These should be protected by bulletproof glass so an intruder can't shoot them out. These can be used for general school information as well. In an emergency a siren, strobe, or flashing light above the board can be used to attract attention. The message could warn students of anything from a fire to a shooter, and pinpoint where the problem is located. These are especially helpful in open campuses, such as large high schools and colleges.

Some schools are considering mounting speakers on three or four tall poles around campus to broadcast to students and staff outside the building and keep them in the loop and out of harm's way.

Bullhorns, while somewhat primitive compared to other technological tools, have been effective in certain emergencies where electricity has been shut off. When dealing with large noisy crowds, they might be indispensable.

- **Does everyone know what specific jobs or tasks he is responsible for?**

  We all hope that the local police, fire, and emergency personnel will respond rapidly and are equipped to handle emergencies. What happens until they get there? Within the building, faculty must have assigned roles to step into until the professionals arrive. This could include sector captains who are in charge of sections of the building. There should be someone assigned to assist and move handicapped students. Some staff should be responsible for checking bathrooms, lockers, and corridors, and all other locations.

  Having staff in strategic locations is important at all times, not just during an emergency. Experience shows that having a teacher in the hall while students change classes reduces bullying, fights, and other types of trouble. Students' behavior is better when they see adults around.

  Making sure all personnel know their roles in an emergency means they can respond more quickly to dangerous situations.

- **What about technology?**

  What technology is available, how can it help, and what should be purchased now? Technology should never be used in lieu of teacher training, but it does have its place in school security. There are thousands of products on the market—some are a waste of money, some are good, and some are essential. Funding is always a problem for schools, and this affects security as well. So when your team meets, you must discuss your major concerns, establish your priorities, and talk with law enforcement and security professionals about how to get the most bang for the buck.

Whatever security problems you uncover, surely someone has faced them before and possibly found solutions for them. Ask around and learn from other schools; it is cheaper (and more reliable) than trial and error.

In 1991, the U.S. Department of Education requested help from a group of security experts from the Security Systems and Technologies Center (SSTC) at Sandia National Laboratories in Albuquerque, New Mexico. The SSTC team visited more than 120 schools over seven years to see what issues most concerned educators. Sandia Labs dedicated more than 150 of its more than 8,000 scientific staff to the research and development of security technologies for schools. The result of this effort was called *The Appropriate and Effective Use of Security Technologies in U.S. Schools.* The Sandia Lab manual made many suggestions (many are in use at airports, courts, and critical locations), but here are just a few recommended for the schools:

o   Restricting access to campus both for cars and pedestrians; requiring vehicle parking stickers to park on campus; making better use of fences and barriers
o   Installing cameras and posting notices that the campus is under visual surveillance
o   Employing guards and roving security
o   Restricting entrance to buildings, and using both portal and handheld metal detectors
o   Requiring the use of picture ID cards for staff and students
Depending on their needs, problems, and funding, schools will pick and choose from these recommendations what they want. One school district where I offered school safety training in the past year that had some serious violence issues dropped their security staff from 16 to 10 for the year because of funding problems.

Detection is another area where technology might be part of the solution. This might include installation of an intrusion-detection system in all hallways, administrative offices, and rooms with high value assets. Use of drug- and bomb-detection dogs (no, they are not the same) should also be considered. Weapon screenings are more common in many schools these days using either portals, handheld detectors, or a combination of both.

Personal alarm systems carried by staff members can produce a loud, piercing noise when activated. These could also be helpful in stopping fights because of the startle effect. Plus they attract other staff members to the incident. They could also function as a GPS device to locate problem spots in the building.

Many schools have already added cameras to key locations and on buses, which have been successful to some degree in reducing fights in the hallways and on the buses. Schools that have installed cameras have experienced a decrease in hallway fights, violence, and vandalism. This is the next best thing to having a teacher present. Cameras, while not necessarily a deterrent to spree shooters, could help locate and identify perpetrators and then provide administrators and law enforcement with intelligence. Some camera systems are computer accessible and will allow local law enforcement to tap in and identify problems in the building when (or even before) they start (e.g., a shooting or riot). These same systems might allow teachers in a locked-down classroom to view cameras around the building so they know where the killer is. Be aware that tech-savvy students may take over the school camera system to monitor the building for themselves (as terrorists typically do). Have a plan in place to deactivate the system from the outside should it be necessary.

In addition to video cameras, the addition of smart-camera technology can help detect suspicious people and situations, and alert campus security or police. Cameras are available that can do identity analysis using facial recognition software to point out those who should not be on campus: students who have been expelled or suspended, known gang members, or drug pushers. This might also include adults who have been ordered by the courts to stay away from students or staff members. Position a camera at all entrances and where guests sign in, thereby providing a record of who came and went.

It's a good idea to have high-intensity flashlights on hand. Power failure might result from a variety of crises. If the sprinklers are set off, they could cause electrical failures. Certain areas of the school might be very dark or impassable. Having high-intensity flashlights could be very helpful. And, as pointed out earlier, such lights can be used to temporarily blind a shooter, buying time for escape or attack.

The Ballistic Transformer, offered by Protective Products International, is a relatively new and versatile ballistic blanket, made from Level IIIA ballistic materials, that can protect one to two people. It could be used to shield students as they are being evacuated from a classroom. In addition, a part of it, the Safety Circle, can be used as a bomb blanket or a gurney to move a wounded person. Every school should have at least one or two. They can be provided to police as they enter the building or used by staff members in response to student violence.

Mechanical doors or gates dropping from the ceiling could cut off or contain an armed intruder. These could drop from the ceiling in various hallways and prevent free movement throughout the building. These should be controlled from the central office and tied to cameras around the building to alert administrators when to trigger them.

- **What about faculty carrying guns on campus?**
Some school districts and colleges have wrestled with the issue of allowing staff members with carry permits to bring weapons on campus. Because of its concern for school safety and the distance from the closest police outpost, a school district in Texas is currently contemplating allowing their staff to do this. Considering the number of students and staff in a building, I have a major concern for collateral damage.

Suggestions for the Educational Community

Law enforcement and military personnel have experienced situations where people get killed or injured by "friendly fire," and these professionals were trained for the stress of combat. I wouldn't trust someone to function in a stressful encounter based solely on his having a carry permit. Can you imagine the confusion when law enforcement arrives and finds staff members running around with guns? How do the police distinguish the good guys from the bad guys? In this case, the cure might be worse than the problem.

DANGEROUS ASSUMPTIONS

Educators, students, or parents often make dangerous assumptions that could result in injuries. The following are the most common I have encountered.

Dangerous Assumption #1: You can't get hurt because the student is "only a kid." In a state of frenzy, an individual's strength can easily double. Added to that, these kids often don't know what they are doing and are out of control. Their strength is then focused on extreme violence and not the controlled force that the teacher might execute. They can definitely hurt you regardless of size, not to mention the weapon in their hand.

Dangerous Assumption #2: The student won't hurt you because he knows you. When out of control, students might not even recognize you. Or they might not like you, despite what you think. While there have been cases where students have come to the aid of a teacher in distress, the teacher might be the target of the killer, even a teacher who has tried to help a student in the past.

Dangerous Assumption #3: They will not hurt you because you are the teacher or principal or whoever. This comes under the heading of presumed compliance discussed earlier: because you are in charge, they will listen to you. Assaults on teachers and administrators occur much more frequently today.

Surviving a Massacre, Rampage, or Spree Killing

DANGEROUS TACTICS

Assumptions aren't the only things that can be dangerous and lead to injury or death. Often when action is taken, the tactics employed are more dangerous than effective.

Dangerous Tactic #1: Attempting to control a violent youth or break up a fight alone. Even law enforcement professionals are told to wait for backup. Plus law enforcement has nonlethal tools (e.g., pepper spray, Taser, baton) to assist them. Lastly, they also have lethal force if needed.

Dangerous Tactic #2: Rushing when speed is not necessary. Things often look worse than they are. A life-and-death scenario is rare in school, but even in a worst-case scenario, it is better to move cautiously, to look and listen, and gather information that can be forwarded to the main office or law enforcement. Verbal intervention and personal presence can often be used, but if you are alone, physical intervention is very dangerous.

Dangerous Tactic #3: Relaxing before the threat has passed. If there is a lull in the action, it is often assumed to be over. This is not always the case. The attacker might be triggered to go off again. As time passes and the violence cues diminish, it is hard to stay alert and ready for action. You can easily get lulled into a sense of calm. Don't let this happen to you.

CONCLUSION

Sooner or later, there will be a call to police from a school, "Help! Get here right away!" Doesn't it make sense to be proactive and minimize the need for calling the police? Increased cooperation between the educational and law enforcement communities will go a long way toward preventing future school violence. This cooperation benefits all.

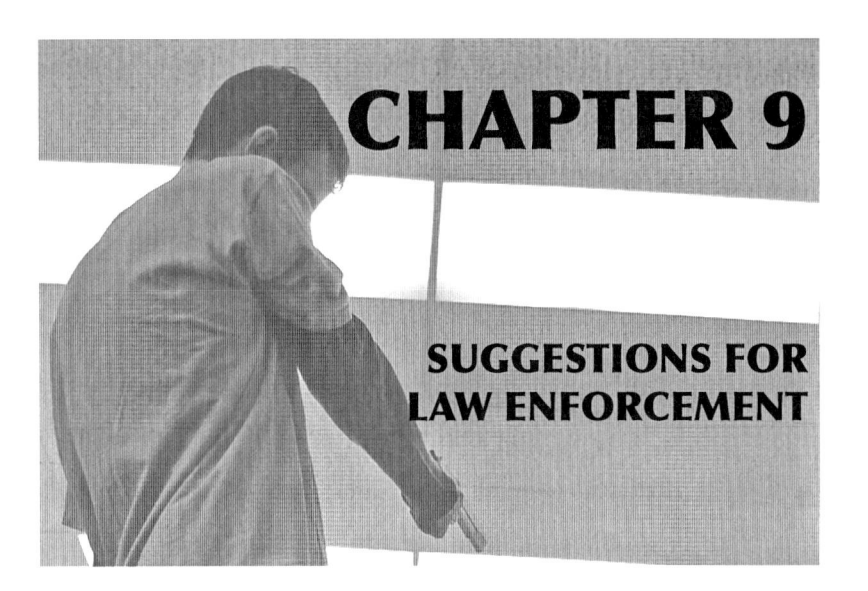

CHAPTER 9

SUGGESTIONS FOR LAW ENFORCEMENT

This chapter is not intended to be an answer to all the problems facing the law enforcement community. Instead, it offers some proactive suggestions for dealing with spree killings. I have worked with the law enforcement community since the early 1980s, and I have spoken at well over 60 national and international law enforcement conferences on a variety of safety topics, so I have a good idea of what is happening out there.

The role of law enforcement becomes more complex by the day. First responders need to be both generalists and specialists at the same time. In terms of spree killings, more has been placed on their shoulders because they will be the first professionals on the scene, and time is of the essence. These factors bring additional risks, which require additional training.

LAW ENFORCEMENT'S ROLE IN SCHOOL VIOLENCE

Before Columbine, the law enforcement community was split about how best to deal with an ongoing rampage shooting. Many preferred to deal with an active shooter the way they handled a hostage or barricade situation: setting up a perimeter, gathering intelligence, and waiting for a negotiator and SWAT team. This makes tactical sense when dealing with a violent confrontation because you want to know what you are dealing with before taking action. However, as Columbine showed, the rampage timetable is so short it doesn't allow the luxury of waiting. The timeline for Columbine was somewhere between 19 and 22 minutes, and this is longer than most school shootings, which average between five and seven minutes from start to finish. In contrast, the average SWAT response is 50 minutes.

Role of First Responder

As a result, Columbine changed the way law enforcement responds to an active shooting at a school, workplace, or public venue. The single most important lesson learned from Columbine is the concept of time. There is no time to wait for SWAT. First responders must engage immediately.

There is more bad news for law enforcement. Calls to 911 usually come in *after* the first shots are fired. Therefore, the first responder on the scene after a 911 call is often beyond the seven-minute window, so most shootings are over before police arrive. In the few cases where police were able to engage the shooter, it was only because officers were already at or near the scene.

While the quick-entry approach is now the accepted procedure, it is fraught with danger for first responders and hostages. Since every second counts, first responders often rush in without ballistic vests or other safety equipment. They also frequently enter the building without knowing much about the situation, such as how many attackers there are or how they are armed (e.g., handguns, assault rifles, bombs, knives, booby traps). They also may be unaware of the number of students in the building, whether any have been taken hostage, and whether the attacker or students inside have put up barricades. This places first responders at a big disadvantage.

Need for Constant Training for Police and Schools

In the future, we are likely to see active shooters become increasingly sophisticated as they study the reports of previous school shootings. They will constantly improve their tactics and become better at countering the efforts of police. Therefore, it is imperative that police officers upgrade their training in dealing with rampage killings. When funding is tight, however, we all know that training often gets reduced drastically. Too many department administrators don't recognize the importance of having their trainers stay up on the latest strategies and tactics. Therefore, it is important for the trainers to educate their administrators.

Unless things change, the response-time factor will remain a major problem facing law enforcement. Some school campuses and buildings are quite large, so getting to the location of the shooter can take valuable time. We hope the first responder has some knowledge of the building, but unfortunately that is too often not the case. It is critical for police to be familiar with (or at least have access to documents of) the floor plans of school buildings in their area. This can't be accomplished during a crisis because time lost equals lives lost. This must be done before a crisis occurs.

This reinforces the need to train school staff and students as to how to survive those initial minutes between when the attack begins and when help arrives. This training should be done by (or at least with the participation of) law enforcement. To do this, schools and law enforcement must improve their collaboration. Educators need to have certain information available when the first responder arrives: who, what, and where. In addition, the school should also have available for the first responder a ballistic transformer protective shield and a layout of the building. In some cases, the school might be able to provide police with live-feed camera footage throughout the building.

School Resource Officer

As I discussed earlier, having cops on the premises is one the most effective actions schools can take to combat violence. Such an officer not only acts as a deterrent to crime but is ready to step in instantly should a violent attack occur. Initially, SROs have had to overcome resistance from both educators and the public about a greater police presence in schools. In most cases, once the initial resistance waned, school officials have responded positively to their presence.

Offer Law Enforcement Services at Schools

While the following suggestions might not have much impact on spree killings, just getting students to view the police in a different light is important. Having officers visit schools regularly shows the human and helpful side of law enforcement—and officers get an inside look at the school building.

Programs currently being offered by local police agencies include drug and alcohol education, school safety planning, abusive parents, and "citizens on patrol," which act as eyes and ears for the police. If students spot any trouble, they call in on special police radios and help is on its way. Plus, there are many other programs in various schools across the nation. I suggest that schools contact their local law enforcement agencies to see how they can take advantage of these safety-oriented programs.

We are slowly approaching the point where the number of violent actions that require a police response could exceed the ability of agencies to respond to them all. Since it is often impossible to tell the difference between a false alarm and the real deal, law enforcement could easily become overwhelmed. What happens at that point? Educators will be on their own, and that is a frightening thought.

Here are some tips for police agencies to increase the odds that officers would be near a school in an emergency.

- Have officers spend downtime (report writing) during the day parked at or near a school.

- Have school personnel ride with police during school hours to locate truant young people and bring them back to school. Newport News, Virginia, has had much success with such a program.

- Have police do random walk-throughs of schools once or twice a week. Police presence does provide an increased feeling of safety and deterrence. Use K-9s on your inspections as a deterrent to bringing drugs, guns, or bombs on campus. Another option is the Quantum Sniffer, a device used by the military to detect a variety of explosives. It is capable of detecting many more items than a dog can. Unlike a dog, the Sniffer can detect both drugs and explosives.

Probation Officers

This saddens me to have to say, but some schools actually have either a part-time or full-time probation officer to oversee the number of juvenile clients in public schools. So far, the program has had some success: lower dropout rates and fewer behavioral problems. When problem students realize that there are some "real" consequences for their misbehavior, they are more apt to toe the line. The probation officer can be a real asset to police officers, especially in terms of who the troublemakers are and what activities they favor.

Monitoring Off-Campus Events

Another problem is that many off-campus events are the setting for violent acts. Sporting events, concerts, and proms have all been the scenes of fights, stabbings, shootings, and riots. Bringing together a large group of emotionally charged (and often drug- or alcohol-fueled) young people can lead to the unexpected. Any events of this nature require planning of which the law enforcement community should be a part.

Restraining Students

For officers (or anyone working in a school), it might be necessary to get involved in physically controlling a violent individual. Using the least amount of force and causing the least possible injury are critical when dealing with children for ethical and legal reasons. The ISC Control Points program would be a great tool for this.

Dr. Les Knight, publisher of the *Defensive Tactics Newsletter* (DTN), developed this program with the assistance of martial artists, police officers, and medical specialists. The ISC Control Points program uses 16 control (or pressure) points to apply low-level force to subdue a resistant subject while minimizing the risk of permanent injury. This medically documented program complements other defensive tactics or techniques being utilized. I have worked with this program since 1996 and highly recommend its use. For more information about ISC Control Points, check out http://www.isccontrol-points.com.

ROLE OF POLICE IN WORKING WITH THE PUBLIC

Engaging the public is not always an easy job. With budgets being trimmed, money must be prioritized, and it is often difficult for police department supervisors to find the money to work these areas. However, some departments have recognized the importance of involving the public. Some departments are training and using "auxiliary police" volunteers to put more eyes and ears on the ground in the community.

Auxiliary members are trained and then directed to ride around communities and report anything out of the ordinary. Another example is the Community Emergency Response Team (CERT) being implemented by Polk County, Florida. They provide a variety of training to volunteers, including disaster preparedness, fire safety, emergency first aid, search and rescue, terrorism, and hazardous materials. The training is provided by police, fire, and emergency services. The county targets community members, businesses, school staff, civic clubs and organizations, various religious groups, and amateur radio operators for this training. In essence they are also putting out many more "eyes and ears" into the community to provide valuable information. In the event of an emergency, they have people trained to assist emergency services with injured parties. More departments should get involved in this type of activity. Contact your local police department to see if it has any such public safety programs in your community.

One example of how the public can help avert a massacre occurred in July 2007 in New York City. An Arab man living in Brooklyn notified the police that his roommates had bombs in their apartment and planned to detonate them soon. The two roommates were angry about the Palestinian situation and planned to detonate the bombs in a crowded subway terminal during rush hour. The suspects had made five bombs, which they intended to use to kill as many Jews as possible and to set off in the subway.

CONCLUSION

If we reflect on the poor job our government (at all levels) did in response to Hurricane Katrina—even with advance warning—what can we expect in a surprise attack on a school, office building, mall, or restaurant? A lot of work has to be done, and even then the experts suggest that there will be casualties and fatalities.

The law enforcement community has a tough job ahead and will require public assistance in the form of information to help prevent future rampages. Agencies and officers must reach out to the public and offer training.

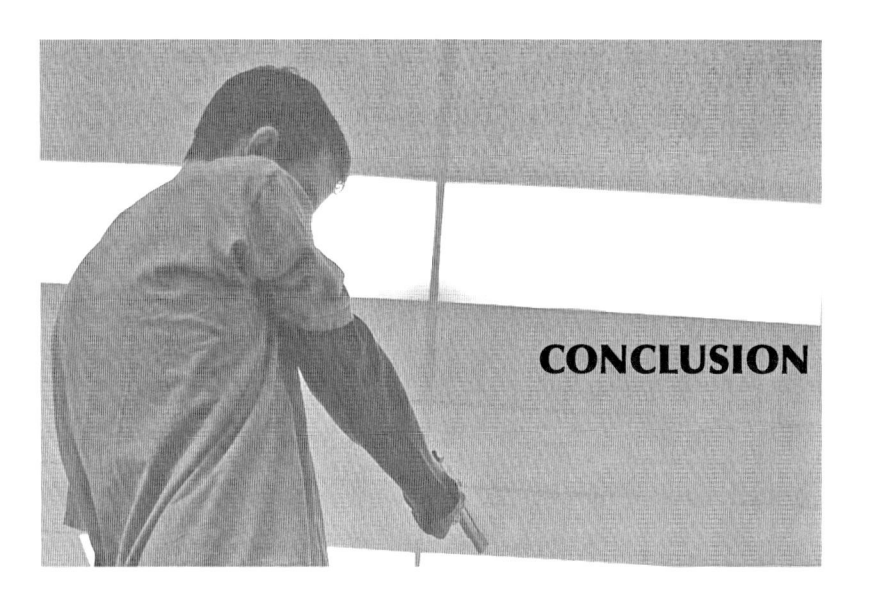

CONCLUSION

"If past practice is any indication of future behavior, we have a violent future ahead."

—Sgt. Paul Ruffolo,
Author of *Violence in America*

This says it all. There are many emotionally disturbed people out there who are ready, willing, and able to get violent at a moment's notice. In addition, they have plenty of previous spree killers to serve as role models.

War and violence take their toll on all of us. Look around the world and see the many places where kids are growing up in an environment of hostility, violence, and fear. A study of urban children found that many suffer from post-traumatic stress disorder because of the climate of fear and violence in their own communities. This eventually produces quite a few potential killers, of others or themselves.

Child abuse in this country is also taking a toll on our youth, and not enough is being done to eliminate it. The dysfunctional family, the media, and video games are all contributing to the problem. Doctors, nurses, teachers, and law enforcement professionals are "mandated reporters" and are required to make a report if they believe abuse or neglect is reasonably suspected. Is it necessary for these people to be trained to know what to look for? Of course, it is.

As stated, one part of the problem is that the law and constitution prevent us from arresting people for what they might do. I see no remedy for this. The gunman in the 2008 Finnish school shooting, who killed 10 people and himself, posted his threat on YouTube. The police brought him in and questioned him, but he was released for lack of evidence. After the shooting, officers discovered that he had been planning this attack for six years. And he was not an anomaly: we see this scenario over and over, with threats made over the Internet. If we can't take action to prevent someone from doing something horrific, I question our ability to stop other such attacks.

The rules governing a democratic society often put its members at risk. Law enforcement agencies have reams of rules and regulations about what they can and can't do. While I understand that we don't want to live in a totalitarian or police state, many of these rules, put in place as a knee-jerk reaction to a specific event or abuse, are creating a situation that handicaps police and enables evil to succeed.

PUBLIC APATHY

Apathy is alive and well and comes in many forms. Could this apathy be partly due to listening to our leaders telling us how safe we are? Many mayors tell you that the crime rate in their city has gone down. Could this have anything to do with promoting tourism in their city? Does this have anything to do with the pressure placed on law enforcement sectors to sanitize crime statistics and minimize the extent of crime? I believe so. After all, we know that school officials doctor violence statistics on their campuses.

The media often belittles any efforts to highlight threats to our public safety. For example, a few years ago the Department of Homeland Security suggested that we have duct tape and plastic sheeting on hand in case of a gas attack. Comics had a field day with that in-

Conclusion

formation. The public is told to be alert, but we aren't told what to be alert for.

This is only part of the problem. I have seen a broad spectrum of public apathy in connection with my safety seminars. Despite the fact that many of the programs are free, the programs are poorly attended, whether the focus is on women's safety, senior safety, or school safety. Several corporations and schools have told me that they don't want to "frighten anyone" and have either declined to do a seminar or asked me not to talk about hostage taking and spree killings. It appears politicians, educators, and corporate leaders are more concerned about frightening the public than providing training that could save lives.

PREVENTION

Obviously not all mass shootings are preventable. However, some might be with everyone's cooperation. How can I be so sure? Because it has already happened. Here are some things that need to be done, besides just using common sense.

We first need to educate the public in a standard operating procedure for evaluating potential threats. In many incidents where people knew something or should have known something, they were just not sure to whom (or how) to report suspicious behavior. There seemed to be no mechanism for reporting this information. You can't call 911 just because you think something "suspicious" is going on or someone might do something. Otherwise, 911 would be overwhelmed, and real-time emergencies might go unanswered. Additionally, often there are no guidelines for what activity should be reported, what action to take once it has been reported, or what agency is responsible. Do a little research or call your local police department to find out who you should call to report suspicious behavior. Disseminate this information to other members of your family and community, and advise the police department to also make this information better known.

Surviving a Massacre, Rampage, or Spree Killing

Assisting Law Enforcement

Law enforcement alone can't do the job of preventing future attacks. They do not have enough eyes and ears available. They need the help of the public, including educators, health-care professionals, parents, and students. Teach kids that if a friend tells you he is going to commit suicide or kill someone, then they must tell a trusted adult. We must show them that this is not violating a trust or ratting out friends. If that works for kids, it should work for adults as well.

With all the preparation a killer goes through to plan an event, somebody might become alarmed over some aspect. This might include the gun dealer, a hardware store, a camera store, a teacher, friends, or family members.

REMAINING ALERT

I have always been a believer in proactive prevention and awareness training as the first line of defense. Being alert is like having an ace in the hole. Pay attention to your surroundings and the people in them. Always be aware of exits, potential hiding places, and the location of emergency services in all buildings you go in. Whenever possible, avoid areas known to be dangerous. Be alert to bizarre or unusual behavior, which can include depression, and then alert security, police or school officials, or office supervisors at work, when you feel uncomfortable. While no one red flag (e.g., amassing firearms and ammunition, weapons training, fascination with violent video games) will single out someone as a potential spree killer, it should be enough to prompt a closer look. Let the professionals make the final decision.

YOU ARE RESPONSIBLE FOR YOUR SAFETY

I am a firm believer in not relying on others to keep me or my family safe during an emergency. For more than 45 years, I have focused my attention on unarmed combat for various reasons. First, un-

Conclusion

armed combat requires a solid base of skills/attributes (e.g., balance, coordination, stamina, flexibility), which ensures a fundamentally solid and versatile foundation for self-defense. Second, even if you usually carry a weapon and are proficient in its use, you may need unarmed self-defense techniques if you suddenly find yourself unarmed or disarmed in a dangerous situation. Plus, even if you have a weapon, in the heat of combat you may be unable to deploy it or retain control of it during the attack. Third, the psychological benefit of knowing you can do what needs to be done, without a weapon, goes a long way toward enabling you to do whatever it takes to survive.

ARE YOU READY?

Are you prepared to recognize a threat developing in your immediate area? Are you able to take appropriate action to protect yourself and those under your charge? Can you do what you need to in order to survive? By reading this book, you have shown that you are interested in improving your chances. Now you just need to follow through. I hope that you never need the information herein; but if you do, I pray that it proves beneficial. Lives are at stake.

Training is an ongoing process, and you must continue to learn from whatever sources are available. Evil never rests, and neither should you.

Stay safe!

GLOSSARY

adrenaline—The hormone of combat, or the fight-or-flight hormone. Also known as epinephrine, it is released by two small glands called the adrenal glands located above the kidneys. The release is triggered by a part of the brain called the amygdala. It is released when danger threatens or in an emergency. Loud noises and bright lights can also trigger its release. Some effects include increased heart rate, increased respiration, elevated blood sugar, and increased blood flow to the brain and major muscles.

amygdala—A primeval arousal center in the brain that can be triggered by powerful emotions, such as fear or anger. When aroused, the amygdala triggers the responses associated with fight or flight, and prompts the release of adrenaline and other hormones into the blood. The response to this trigger can disrupt the control of rational thought.

autonomic nervous system (ANS)—A branch of the central nervous system (brain and spinal cord) that helps people adapt to changes in their environment. This is your first line of defense to threats until the endocrine system (adrenal glands and hormones) kicks in. The ANS adjusts some functions in response to stress and threats by regulating blood vessel size and blood pressure, heart rate, and respiration.

complex motor skills—One of the three groups of motor skills: gross, fine, and complex. Complex motor skills involve the coordination of many muscle groups, and require hand-eye coordination, timing, tracking, and other skills acting in concert. Under high levels of stress, complex motor skills are unreliable and likely to fail. Many martial arts self-defense techniques fall into this category, and while they might look impressive in a competition, they will likely fail in a real-life situation.

concealment—Any object that would block a shooter's view of a target. Bullets, especially larger caliber or rifle shots, will penetrate most objects, including doors and most walls. While these objects conceal you, they don't provide the protection from bullet penetration.

cover—Any object that would stop or deflect bullets. Cover serves to both hide and protect. Steel, stone, Kevlar shield, or sand embankments could offer cover by deflecting, if not stopping, bullets. Most people don't recognize the penetrating ability of many rounds.

emotionally disturbed person (EDP)—A person suffering from the standard psychological definitions of paranoia, schizophrenia, and other mental disorders. It also includes anyone acting out violently because of extreme hate, revenge, or rage. The problem with many EDPs is that their symptoms aren't visible and their behavior is often seen as harmless. It is only after an event that many of the red flags become visible.

fight or flight—Hyperarousal or the acute stress response is the body's primitive, automatic, genetically hard-wired response that

Glossary

prepares the body to fight or flee from a perceived attack. Fainting or freezing are two additional responses that are often not mentioned (also called the fright, fight, or flight response).

fine motor skills—One of the three groups of motor skills. Fine motor skills require great coordination between muscle groups and hand-eye coordination. They tend to fail under high levels of stress.

flinch or startle response—The body's reaction to an unexpected stimulus, such as a loud noise, quick movement near the head, or flash of light. Flinching consists of two phases: an initial startle response and a longer defensive response directed toward protection from the threat. In the latter stage there are typically three hand positions. If the attack is close from the front, the hands are placed up in front of the body. If the attack is from the front at a distance, the hands are up but extended outward. If the attack is sudden from the side or the attacker overwhelms the defender, the back is turned and the hands are brought up to cover the back of the head. Essentially the goal of the flinch response is to protect the head and brain.

fragile person—A person who tends to be covertly disturbed and potentially explosive. Such people tend to function well until some problem arises.

funneling—A technique that creates a choke point, using a narrow passage such as a doorway, where only one person of a group can enter at a time. This is a good tactic to employ when facing multiple attackers. However, it could be a major problem when trying to escape in a large group, which could cause people to be crushed.

gross motor skills—The group of motor skills that utilizes large muscle groups and emphasizes simple responses (e.g., knees and elbows). These techniques are best suited and most reliable under high levels of stress.

hypervigilance—A temporary freezing when caught by surprise whose purpose is to detect possible threats and scan the environment for the source of the threat.

lone wolf—An individual working alone without affiliation to a specific group who plans an attack against an individual or group. He is often influenced by Internet websites designed to incite hatred or violence. This is a tactic of the white supremacist movement.

100 percent rule—The rule that no tactic, plan, or course of action works all the time. The more we know about survival, the better the chances that we select a tactic that has a high degree of success.

psychology of blame—A tactic developed by many groups to blame their lack of success on others. This is often used to indoctrinate children. Unfortunately, it creates a self-fulfilling prophecy for many and reinforces prejudices, hostility, and sometimes violence.

scanning—The ability to spot things anywhere in our field of vision. Once the body is under stress or threat of attack, scanning immediately switches to tunnel vision, which focuses on the threat or danger exclusively.

suicide by cop—The strategy used by some people to commit suicide by having a police officer shoot and kill them.

sympathetic nervous system (SNS)—The part of the autonomic nervous system that triggers the fight-or-flight response when a person feels threatened.

Glossary

tactical breathing—A technique used by law enforcement, the military, and martial artists to deactivate a sympathetic nervous system (SNS) mass discharge and return the body to homeostasis (normal). The exercise involves breathing in for a count of three, holding your breath for a count of three, and exhaling (while compressing the diaphragm) for a count of three. This exercise is done until your heart rate is reduced to a level where you are able to perform at your optimum. It usually requires three sets to be effective.

targeted violence—A term developed by the Secret Service to refer to any violent incident where a known attacker selects a specific person (e.g., a particular classmate, teacher, coworker) or location (e.g., post office, factory, federal office building).

Tueller drill—A self-defense training exercise created by Sgt. Dennis Tueller in the mid-1980s. It established that the average person can cover 21 feet in 1.5 seconds. This has serious implications for someone facing a goal-oriented knife attacker or running during a spree shooting because it correlates distance with time.

tunnel vision—A narrowing of the field of vision in response to a threat. As soon as a threat is perceived, we tend to focus our view on the threat. Our overall field of vision diminishes, and other threats might not be seen.

BIBLIOGRAPHY

Arnspiger, B. "Train for Survival," *Police* (November 1998).

Aviv, Juval. (2004). *Staying Safe: The Complete Guide to Protecting Yourself, Your Family and Your Business,* Harper Resource.

Bacon, T. "Train Assaults," *Tactical Response* (Fall 2003): 44–46.

Bartlett, D. "In the Crosshairs," *Police* (March 2004).

Basich, Melanie."TREXCO West 2009: Keynote Speakers Scoff at Politicians' Claims of End to War on Terror," *Police* (May 2009): 20–21.

Brandley, P., Jr. "Active Shooter's Forgotten Factor," *Law and Order* (June 2007*):* 52–59.

———. "Active Shooter's Forgotten Factor," *Tactical Response* (March–April 2008)*:* 54–59.

Bronson, S. "Terrorists Try to Beat SWAT," *Law and Order* (March 2003).

Surviving a Massacre, Rampage, or Spree Killing

Buice, E. "Crisis Communications: Competency Is Critical." *Law and Order* (November 2002).

Burroughs, W.E. "Hostage Rescue: Bus and Airplane Assaults." *Police and Security News* (November–December 1996).

Cahallans, W. "Rolling Thunder Active Shooter," *Tactical Response* (March–April 2008): 38–43.

Challans, B. "We Are Not Ready," *Tactical Response* (March–April 2008): 79.

Cobb, Eric, and Rob Pincus. "The S.P.E.A.R. System and Converting the Flinch Response," *Law and Order* (October 2003): 150–158.

Cohen, Arthur. *"Become Streetwise!" A Woman's Guide to Personal Safety*, Target Consultants, NY, 2003.

———. "Body Language: Are Cops Pre-programmed for Failure?" *Defensive Tactics Newsletter* (January 1997): 1, 3.

———. "Is There a Need for a Permanent Police Presence in Schools?" *Defensive Tactics Newsletter* (April 2005): 5–6.

———. "Ready or Not: Fight Intervention Strategies," *Middle School Companion* (January–February 1997): 6, 8.

———. "Stopping Fights in School: One of Education's Dark Little Secrets," *Defensive Tactics Newsletter* (May 2007): 5–6.

———. "Why Schools Are Likely to See More Riots in the Future," *Law Enforcement Executive Forum* (August 2008): 11–17.

Bibliography

Cormier, B. "Four Killed in Argentina High School Shooting," *Newsday* (September 29, 2004).

Davis, Kevin. "Active Shooter Deployment Bags," *Tactical Response* (September–October 2008): 70–72.

———. "Up Close, Personal, and Violent," *Police* (September 2006): 56–59.

Douglas, D. "Jumping Into the Fire," *Police* (October 2002).

Duncan, S. "Pre-incident Behavior of Active Shooters," *Law and Order* (June 2008): 69–74.

Fairburn, R., and D. Grossman. "Preparing for School Attacks," Killogy Research Group (April 17, 2007): 1–5.

Fisher, M. "8 Years Later, Nothing Has Changed," *Newsday* (April 20, 2007): A51.

Floreno, Jeff. "Winning Ways to Secure Schools," *Law & Order* (June 2009): 65–70.

Garner, G. Capt. "Smart Approaches to Off-duty Intervention," *Police* (January 1997): 34–37, 68.

Giduck, J. "Are Terrorists Targeting Our Schools?" *Police* (September 2006).

Griffith, David. "Cleaning Out My Files," *Police* (April 2009): 8.

———. "The Fallacy of the Nonviolent Offender," *Police* (September 2009): 8.

Surviving a Massacre, Rampage, or Spree Killing

———. "Finding a Cure for a Cancer," *Police* (March 2009): 14.

———. "Stopping the Next 9/11," *Police* (September 2008): 46–53.

———."Terrorism with a Small 't,'" *Police* (July 2009): 8.

———. "Unarmed Victim Zones," *Police* (December 2009): 8.

———. "You Would Have Shot Back," *Police* (January 2009): 8.

"Gunfire Kills 4 in Kansas City." *Newsday* (April 30, 2007): A-19.

Hamilton, M. "Can We Stop the Next Cho Seung-Hui?" *Police* (June 2007): 48–50.

Hammond, Peter Dr. (2008, April 21). "Slavery, Terrorism, and Islam," Front Page Magazine.Com.

"Hate Group Numbers Surge." *Southern Poverty Law Center Report* (Spring 2009): 1.

Hoffman, J. "Is There Too Much SWAT?" *Law and Order* (September 1998).

Hollowell, P. "Active Shooter Prevention Matrix," *Law and Order* (June 2008): 79–83.

Isaacs, Richard. "What Constitutes Suspicious Behavior and What to Do About It," *Lubrinco E-News* (2007).

Janich, M. "Beyond the Tueller Drill," *Police* (November 2008): 60–65.

Jones, K. "Terrorism Deterrence, Part II," *Tactical Response* (March–April 2007): 44–46.

Bibliography

———. "Terrorism Deterrence, Part III," *Tactical Response* (May–June 2007): 30–31.

———. "Terrorism Deterrence, Conclusion," *Tactical Response* (January–February 2008): 30–32.

Katz, S. "Bus Assault Course," *Law and Order* (March 2002): 93–96.

———. "Spain's GEO Bus Assault Training." *Law and Order* (September 2002).

Kelleher, Jennifer Sinco. "Columbine: 10 Years Later," *Newsday* (April 19, 2009): A-18-A19.

Keller, Larry. "From Hate to Hurt," *SPLC Intelligence Report* (Summer 2009): 50–54.

Kingsbury, Alex. "The War on Gangs," *U.S. News and World Report* (December 15, 2008): 33–36.

Klein, A. "Va. District Hit Hard by Graduate's Killing Spree," *Education Week* (April 25, 2007).

Linett, Howard. "Why You Aren't Being Trained to Prevent Terror Attacks," *Police* (September 12, 2008): 12.

Manson, Thomas. "CLEAR: Biometric at the Airport," *Law and Order* (June 2008): 28–30.

Maxwell, L. "College Rampage Renews School Safety Concerns," *Education Week* (April 25, 2007): 1, 16–17.

———. "'Copycatting' May Produce More Threats," *Education Week* (April 25, 2007).

Surviving a Massacre, Rampage, or Spree Killing

McBride, James. "Should Campus Police Be Armed?" *Law and Order* (June 2009): 62–64.

McCormack, William, JD. "State and Local Law Enforcement Contributions to Terrorism Prevention," *FBI Law Enforcement Bulletin* (March 2009): 1–7.

McIndoe, B. "The Psychology of Risk," *Mastering T & E Expense Management* (April 2007): 14.

"Mental-Health Disorders Gain Foothold during Teenage Years," *Education Week* (June 22, 2005): 12.

Messer, John. "The Art of Breaking and Raking," *Tactical Response* (September–October 2008): 26–30.

Meyr, E. "European Elite Tactical Units," *Law and Order* (November 1999).

———. "Israeli Response to Hostage Taking," *Law and Order* (March 2002): 40–44.

Morton, A. "Can We Prevent the Next Shooting?" *Washington Post* Metro Section (April 14, 2008): B1.

"Most Police Readers Prepared to Engage School Shooters," *Police* (June 2007): 14.

Mulligan, Bernie. "When Tragedy Struck, School Was Prepared," *New York Teacher* (May 21, 2009): 21.

O'Donnell, E. "What Might Campus Cops Do?" *Newsday* (April 19, 2007).

Bibliography

Oldham, S. "Active Shooter Equipment," *Law and Order* (June 2008): 75–78.

Papa, J. "Criminalizing the Creative," *Newsday* (April 29, 2007): A-56-A-57.

Parent, R. "Surviving a Lethal Threat," *Law and Order* (October 1999).

Parra, Natalia. "Tourists Dive for Cover in Acapulco Shootout," The Associated Press (June 8, 2009).

"Patrol Response Challenge," Special Report: Active Shooter by Law Staff, *Law and Order*: 62–68.

Peak, K., PhD.; E. Radli; C. Pearson; and D. Balaam. "Hostage Situations in Detention Settings: Planning and Tactical Considerations," *FBI Law Enforcement Bulletin* (October 2008): 1–13.

Petrocelli, Joseph. "April Fools: Watch Out This Month for Terrorists, School Shooters, Nazis, and Stoners. It's Their Time of Year," *Police* (April 2009): 20–23.

Pinnizzotto, A., PhD.; E. Davis, MA; and C. Miller III. "Escape from the Killing Zone," *FBI Law Enforcement Bulletin* (July 4, 2004): 1–7.

Pinnizzotto, A. PhD; E. Davis, MA; S. Bohrer, MBA; and R. Cheney. "Law Enforcement Perspective on the Use of Force," *FBI Law Enforcement Bulletin* (April 2009): 16–21.

Pinnizzotto, A., PhD., and George D. Deshazor, LCSW, BCD. "Interviewing Erratic Subjects," *FBI Journal* (November 1997).

Surviving a Massacre, Rampage, or Spree Killing

Pinkerton, J. "We Can't Afford to Be a Nation of Soft Targets," *Newsday* (April 19, 2007).

Polsky, Carol. "More Seek Help in Stressful Time," *Newsday* (April 20, 2009): A4–A5.

"Prisons Clogged with Mentally Ill," *Newsday* (July 4, 2004).

Ramirez, E. "SWAT and the Law," *Police* (May 2003).

Rayburn, Michael. "Survival Is Your Responsibility," *Police* (January 2009): 50–53.

Remsberg, Charles. "Extreme Encounters," *The Law Enforcement Trainer* (Third Quarter, 2004): 9–13.

Rosenbarger, M. "Mock School Shooting," *Law and Order* (December 2001): 30–36.

Rosenthal, R. "Gunman, Hostages, and the Media," *Law and Order* (May 2000).

Samuels, C. "Behavior Disorders in Teens Are Focus of New R & D Effort," *Education Week* (September 3, 2008): 1, 12.

Sanow, E. "Active Shooter: Can't Arrive in Time," *Tactical Response* (November–December 2007): 111.

——————. "Active Shooter: Can't Get There in Time," *Law and Order* (January 6, 2008): 6.

——————. "Live-Fire Building Searches," *Law and Order* (August 1998): 77–82.

Bibliography

Schanlaub, Russ. "School Shootings: A Look Back, a Look Ahead," *Law and Order* (June 2009): 56–60.

Scott, David. "Policing Regional Mass Transit," *FBI Law Enforcement Bulletin* (July 2009): 1–10.

Scoville, Dean. "Shots Fired," *Police* (July 2009): 88–91.

——————. "Five Ways the Economy Will Change Your Job," *Police* (February 2009): 39–43.

——————. "Santa Ana, California 12/27/2006," *Police* (February 2009): 46–49

Siddle, Bruce. "Survival Stress: The Renaissance Man," *Police* (February 2007).

"Slain Neo-Nazi Possessed 'Dirty Bomb' Components." *Southern Poverty Law Center Report* (Spring 2009): 3.

Slatkin, A., EdD. "Intelligence in Crisis and Hostage Negotiations," *Law and Order* (July 2002).

——————. "Suicide Risk and Hostage/Barricade Situations Involving Older Persons," *FBI Law Enforcement Bulletin* (April 2003).

Smith, Scott. "If the Glove Fits," *Police* (July 2009): 54, 56.

Spaulding, D. Lt. "Planning for Tactical Entry," *Police* (April 1997).

Stone, R. "'High Incident': The Making of a Reality-Inspired TV Police Show," *Police* (July 1997): 41–43.

Surviving a Massacre, Rampage, or Spree Killing

Strentz, T. "Terrorism and the Tenants of Islam," *Tactical Response* (May–June 2007): 60–68.

Tactical Response Staff. "Patrol Response Challenge," *Tactical Response* (March–April 2008): 30–36.

—————. "Special Report: Active Shooter, *Tactical Response* (June 2008): 62–68.

Talon, J. "A Fragile Mental Health System," *Newsday* (April 2007).

"Texas Teachers in Independent District Okay to Carry Handguns to School," *Newsday* (August 14, 2008): A15, and the Internet.

Tueller, D. "How CLOSE Is TOO CLOSE?" The Police Policy Studies Council *(*2004) .

Valdez, A. "Home Invasion Robberies," *Police* (August 2002).

Vergakis, B. "Utah Allows Guns on College Campuses," Associated Press (April 27, 2007).

Viadero, Debra. "Lessons Sifted From Tragedy at Columbine," *Education Week* (April 8, 2009): 1, 12–13.

"Victims Were Hit 100 times," Associated Press (April 23, 2007).

"Violent Youth on School Campuses," *Education Week* (September 5, 2001).

Vonk, K. "Police Performance Under Stress," *Law and Order* (August 2008): 86–92.

Bibliography

Vossekuil, B.; M. Reddy, PhD.; and R. Fein, PhD. "Safe School Initiative: An Interim Report on the Prevention of Targeted Violence in Schools," U.S. Secret Service National Threat Assessment Center in Collaboration with the U.S. Department of Education (October 2000): 1–9.

Wagner, Jim Sgt. "Dealing with a Live Grenade," *Black Belt* (March 2002).

———. "The Door Ambush," *Black Belt* (April 2007): 60–62.

———. "Surviving a Massacre," *Black Belt* (November 2005): 48–50.

———. "Timing Is Everything," *Black Belt* (March 2007): 60–62.

Webb, D. "School Walk-Throughs," *Law and Order* (June 2008): 84–86.

Wikipedia."Changes in Police Response" (November 22, 2007).

Williams, George. "Acceptable Casualties Versus Reasonable Risk," *Law and Order* (October 2000).

———. "Re-thinking the 21-Foot Rule," *Tactical Response* (November–December 2005): 26–31.

Williams, George, and Jeff Martin. "Responding to the Active Shooter," *Law and Order* (October 1999).

Winslow, O., and M. Lefkowitz. "Securing Safety," *Newsday* (April 13, 2007): A-4.

"Worries," *Newsday* (April 20, 2007): A7.

Surviving a Massacre, Rampage, or Spree Killing

Yarbaugh, C. "Rapid Deployment for Active Shooters," *Tactical Response* (November–December 2008): 92–94.

Yeager, D. "Resolving Conflicts Between Police and Schools," *Law and Order* (April 2007).

Zagier, A. "Schools Examine Safety Warning Systems," YAHOO! News (April 19, 2007).

ABOUT THE
AUTHOR

Professor Arthur Cohen is a nationally and internationally known personal safety expert. After 33 years as a junior/senior high school science teacher, he designed and taught two graduate courses on school safety for Norwich and Alfred Universities and became a leading spokesman in the field of school safety training. Over the past 25 years, he has taught at dozens of state and national educational conferences. Cohen combines many different perspectives and an array of disciplines to help educators understand, prevent, and cope with school violence.

Cohen's involvement with the law enforcement community dates back to the early 1980s as a member of and instructor for the Justice System Training Association and later with Police Self-Defense Instructors International (PSDII). He became a charter member and frequent staff instructor of the American Society of Law Enforcement Trainers in the mid-1980s and is currently a charter member of the International Law Enforcement Educators and Trainers Association. He has received numerous awards and recognition from members of the law enforcement community, including the 1996 and 2002 Leadership Award from the *Defensive Tactics Newsletter* and the 1990 Award of Excellence from PSDII, and has been listed in multiple editions of *Who's Who in Law Enforcement Training*. He has been a speaker at more than 50 national and international law enforcement conferences and taped a segment on Law Enforcement Television Network.

Cohen martial arts career spans more than 45 years. He is a 6th-degree black belt in taekwon do and has an instructor's certificate in *arnis de mano*, Filipino stick and knife fighting. In the late 1980s, he was a staff member for Long Island University's Karate Instructor's Certificate Program and was part of the center's United States/Long Island University instructional staff that visited and taught at the Yugoslavian Junior Olympic Karate Team summer camp. The martial arts community has recognized his work with numerous awards: Bushido Award, Pioneer in Martial Arts Award, and a nomination for the Budo International Martial Arts Hall of Fame for his outstanding lifetime contribution to personal safety training. A number of years ago, Cohen became an instructor trainer for the ISC Control Point Program and currently serves on the advisory board of both the International Combative Self-Defense Association and Israeli Krav International.

Currently, Cohen designs and teaches programs for The Center for School and Personal Safety Research, a subgroup of Target Consultants International. Because of his innovative work in the areas of personal safety, school safety, police defensive tactics, and martial arts, he often instructs trainers in the personal safety field. He is sometimes referred to as the "Streetwise Professor." He has a bachelor's degree in biology from Hunter College and a master of arts degree from Stony Brook University.